World University L

The World University Library is an international series
of books, each of which has been specially commissioned.
The authors are leading scientists and scholars from all over
the world who, in an age of increasing specialization, see the
need for a broad, up-to-date presentation of their subject.
The aim is to provide authoritative introductory books for
students which will be of interest also to the general
reader. Publication of the series takes place in Britain,
France, Germany, Holland, Italy, Spain, Sweden and
the United States.

Jacques Maquet

Power and Society in Africa

Translated from the French
by Jeannette Kupfermann

World University Library

McGraw-Hill Book Company
New York Toronto

Contents

Preface

When the publishers asked for a book on African sociology in keeping with the rest of their collection, they left the author complete freedom to approach the subject as he thought best. The author chose to present an interpretation of African societal organisations.

An interpretation is based on a description of facts gathered by trained, critical observers; but it goes beyond that, too. It is an intellectual assessment of what links and explains the facts. Like description, interpretation claims to be objective and not imaginary. But its relationship to the 'object' is not the same as in description: the distance is greater, and there are more intermediaries. All this makes it difficult to appreciate the value of an interpretation.

Certain critics, in order to evaluate an intellectual interpretation, look for a rationally satisfying construction – one which explains all the necessary facts in a coherent and elegant (that is, economical) way; and one, too, which conforms to the intellectual climate of the time. For others, the interpretation of facts depends as much on the social and cultural outlook of the author as on the object he is studying, and consequently they ask for a full professional and intellectual profile of him.

It is up to the reader to choose what path of assessment he will. So that he can choose the second if he wishes, the author, before signing off, thinks it might be useful to give the following information.

His first studies were in law, philosophy (his philosophy thesis was devoted to the sociology of knowledge), and then in anthropology. During this formative period, he attended two European universities (Louvain and London), and an American one (Harvard). He lived in Black Africa for some ten years during the colonial period. He belonged to the white caste, but in the rather marginal position of anthropologist. He was director of a research centre in social sciences in the Great Lakes region; then he taught in a Central African university. After leaving Africa, he continued research and teaching at the University of Paris and the University of Brussels, and then in the United States.

Case Western Reserve University
Cleveland, Ohio

1968–9

Note on the spelling and pronunciation of African words

English spelling is used for tribal names which have become part of the language (e.g. Bantu, Zulu, as noun or adjective). The names of African states are spelt according to the usage of their governments (e.g. Zambia, Nigeria, Niger, Rwanda). For names of traditional African peoples and languages a simplified phonetic spelling (without diacritical marks) has been used; words are given in the root form, without the various prefixes by which the Bantu languages distinguish singular and plural and different classes of noun. Thus we say Nkole and not Munyankole, Tutsi (a Tutsi man) and Tutsi customs. Common nouns referring to persons (e.g. *garagu*) or institutions (e.g. *okutoisha*) are treated in the same way but printed in italics.

Pronunciation
In the phonetic spelling adopted
u is pronounced *oo*

e –	–	like *ay* in *say*
w –	–	as in *winter*
s –	–	always as in *so*
g –	–	as in *game*

1 The approach to African societies

In Africa, as indeed throughout the world, an individual's social horizon extends beyond the elementary family of husband, wife, and children; it encompasses everyone with whom he maintains continuous relationships, especially relationships of co-operation; it thus embraces the people with whom he works or plays, is on good terms with, or bad. Each individual has his own social horizon, although the horizons of several persons may overlap, and this is usually what happens in a village.

Social horizon is a subjective concept because it is always described from the point of view of a single individual. But the concept of the village is objective since it is possible to see its reality from the outside as it exists in space (the locality of the village), and in time (its history). However, the subjective and objective aspects of social phenomena are closely linked, since the sum total of the villagers' individual experiences corresponds to an observable social structure. But one cannot always draw a perfect parallel between experiences as they are lived and the units one can observe. It is possible to belong, in a legal sense, to an enormous group comprising tens or even hundreds of millions of people, without any acute awareness of it in one's daily life.

The poles of subjectivity and objectivity indicate only one of the dimensions of social relationships. There are others. One's behaviour differs according to whether the people concerned are young or old, men or women; descended from the same ancestor as oneself, or from others; of a superior, equal, or inferior rank; subject to the same authority or foreigners. Thus men weave innumerable relationships among themselves. These relationships, seen by them to have qualitative differences, are grouped into special categories, and most important of all, are experienced in daily life.

To the sociologist, each of these relationships constitutes a 'fact', a 'given item'. This is the irreducible reality which provides

Fort-Jesus in Mombasa (present-day Kenya) was built
by the Portuguese to guard the port. The work of
building took from 1569 to at least 1593. The masons
came from India, the labour from the nearby town of
Malindi and the architect from Italy.

both his point of departure and the point to which he must return
when testing his hypotheses. But it is not easy to grasp this reality in
both hands, fragmented as it is into myriads of transitory phenomena. For after all, the interaction of two individuals can be a
matter of a mere moment. Confronted with this uneven fabric, this
tangled mass of social relationships which is social reality, the
anthropologist cannot be merely a passive recording instrument;
he must bring into play all the various distinctions, classifications
and groupings, in order to understand that reality.

Africa south of the Sahara

The social reality of the Africa we are considering, that part
situated south of the Sahara, covers an enormous amount of
territory. It is often called 'Black Africa'. The Sahara is not simply
an arbitrary boundary line; it also acts as a frontier between two
different cultural worlds. These two worlds are, however, not
complete strangers to one another. Caravan routes enabled them
to maintain continuous relationships over the centuries, and thus
they exerted a mutual influence on one another. Nonetheless there
are more significant and profound cultural similarities between the
different countries of Black Africa than exist between the latter and
the Africa bordering the Mediterranean. It is on the basis of this
conclusion, arrived at by means of a comparative study, that we
can speak of the existence of a cultural community, an 'africanity'.
It is true that in the contemporary Africa of independence and
industrialisation, cultural differences between the Mediterranean
north and the vast central regions are blurred; but this was not
always the case. We cannot ignore the importance of history.
Léopold Sédar Senghor, who, with Aimé Césaire and Léon Damas,
was one of the originators of the concept of *négritude* during the
years 1932–4, understood it to be the totality of values of the black

peoples. Now, more than thirty years later, Senghor believes that values of the black world complement those of the Arab world[1]. In order for this complementary relationship and convergence to exist, there must be some duality to begin with[2].

If we imagine its history unfolding before us, we must stop at three essential periods which have left their mark on African evolution since the middle of the nineteenth century: the traditional, the colonial, and the independent. The traditional period can be said to have begun when agricultural techniques of production and the domestication of animals became widespread. Before that, as everywhere else, man started out as a hunter and gatherer, depending on nature alone for a livelihood. In the case of Africa, it seems more relevant to think of the prehistoric period as coming to a close with what one calls the Neolithic Revolution (farming and the domestication of animals) rather than with the advent of writing. If one were to adopt the latter criterion, African prehistory would go on almost until the end of the nineteenth century. Such a division of the African past would minimise the importance of the change from techniques of collection to those of production; and it is the latter that is the first step toward the domination of nature. The traditional period was not entirely static: people and their institutions did undergo some change. Unfortunately, we are rarely able to retrace the history of that period. Nonetheless we do have a few clues, thanks to oral traditions and archaeological remains. When we talk about the traditional period we shall, in actual fact, be referring to the last stage before the time when the colonial conquest took place in the nineteenth century.

This conquest, which marks the beginning of the colonial period, is easier to date. In 1885 the Treaty of Berlin laid down the rules for the partition of Africa between the European powers. This can be seen as symbolic of the end of African sovereignty, and as heralding the second great technical revolution that Africa experienced – industrialisation. We can take another symbolic date to mark the end of colonial domination – 1960. The first independent African states, Sudan and Ghana, date back respectively to 1956 and 1957; the movement rapidly expanded, and reached its height in 1960, the year in which seventeen colonial territories became states.

The concept of global societies

Suppose that we attempt to make a synchronic view of the social reality of Africa south of the Sahara, with each of the three periods we have distinguished – a sort of x-ray picture, taking a moment in time from the moving web of social relationships, and fixing it. If we examine this picture a little more closely, we will see first that the social fabric is very patchy: in some places, such as the Equatorial forest and the steppes of the southern hemisphere, the network of social relationships is very stretched, with wide open spaces between the threads. In others, like the high plateaux between Lakes Victoria and Tanganyika and the western shore at the mouth of the rivers Senegal, Niger and Congo, the web is tight, with all its many threads intertwined in every direction.

Looking still more closely, we can distinguish heavy concentrations or knots, where all the threads converge. The further away one gets from these points of convergence the more stretched the fabric becomes: likewise it tightens up again as it approaches another convergence. The pattern of these focal points, varying in their density and proximity to one another, is repeated over the whole surface of the sociological picture of Africa. What is the significance of this?

It means that social relationships are distributed in an unequal fashion; that individuals are assembled in groups in which the members interact more closely and with greater frequency, and

14

The village is the social horizon of all
its inhabitants. A dry savanna village
in the Haute-Volta, isolated but connected
to another similar unit by the road.

certainly not just in a random fashion, since we can see lines of
convergence. The technique of obtaining a social x-ray is, of
course, an imaginary one, but similar results can be obtained by
using quantitative methods of observation. This has never, to be
sure, been applied to anything on the scale of a whole continent. A
social 'map' of this kind would show us how to divide the social
fabric into units that are not arbitrarily chosen.

These clusters of social relationships, separated from one another
by areas of rare and diffuse interraction, correspond to entities
generally known as *global societies*.

As in all societies, there are permanent groups of people with
organised activities; furthermore, the totality of these organised
activities assures the continuity of the group, and meets the vital
needs of its members. The global society is self-perpetuating (it
contains both men and women), maintaining its identity over
several generations (it has institutions which pass on the experience
of the adults to the young), and defending itself from external
dangers as well as internal forces of disintegration. It also provides,
from the point of view of each of its members, a framework for life
from birth to the grave. One can grow up, marry, work and grow
old without even having to 'step outside' one's global society.

The global society is an 'objective' concept in the sense that not
only those who are a part of it, but also neighbours and outside
observers recognise it as such. An isolated global society composed
of a restricted number of members can coincide with the social
horizon of each one of them. But in fact, the social horizon of one
individual usually takes into account only one part of the social
relationships found in his global society. They include, too,
especially in today's world, relationships with members of other
global societies. The concept also incorporates the psychic notion
of *esprit de corps*. A man identifies with his global society; becomes
attached to it and all it stands for, and calls himself Ashanti or

Ganda, Ghanaian or Ugandan. He is identified in the same way by other people.

Since the concept of a global society is independent of the individual criteria of each observer, it is a particularly useful category. Its application to the African reality of the last hundred years gives us some light on an interesting process of social change. There is a break in continuity between the global societies of traditional and present-day Africa, with a few exceptions. In spite of the fact that the global societies of the pre-colonial period were usually permanent, they no longer act today as frameworks of collective life.

Up to the time of the colonial conquest, kingdoms and chiefdoms, tribes and federations of nomad bands were the only human groups that provided their members with conditions which enabled them to live, and to live well. These units, south of the Sahara, numbered over a thousand; one of the best lists enumerates more than 850, and it is not complete[3]. Since the beginnings of colonial rule – sometimes even before the actual occupation of the land – the demarcation and mapping out of zones of influence had taken into account mountains, rivers, even meridians and parallels, but rarely traditional frontiers. These were generally unknown at that time, or seemed obscure to the European mind, accustomed as it was to well-defined boundaries. During the first few years, even the first decades, of the colonial period, the traditional units continued to be the centre of numerous activities; there were always the flow of production and distribution of goods, marriage and hereditary succession, rites and cults performed in a traditional way. From the beginning, only political relations were transferred from kingdoms or tribes to the colonial sphere, where the supreme local authority was the governor. But as time went on, the interactions of colonial subjects overflowed the traditional social framework and extended over the entire colony. As they used the same currency, their commercial relationships potentially, and often actually, covered the length and breadth of the territory; the labour market also expanded; the educational organisation, the judiciary administration, and taxation all constituted uniform systems to which one was subject, regardless of tribal origins. Thus, little by little, a transfer was effected: each individual belonged to two centres of converging social relationships. One was diminishing while the other grew larger without, however, completely replacing the first. In actual fact the individual never identified in the psychological sense with the colonial society. He never thought of it as 'his' society, as a group with which he felt solidarity and was proud to belong. Nevertheless, it was the colonies, not the societies of the traditional period, which became independent.

This indicates the importance of systems of relationship, and their solidity, quite independent of the feelings of attachment of which they may be the basis. Yet without such sentiments, a group cannot completely fulfil the functions of a global society. During the first ten years of their existence, the young states of Black Africa have been forced to take this 'esprit de corps' aspect of global societies into account. As is well demonstrated by secessionist crises, not every state has been successful in inspiring the loyalty of all its citizens.

Societal relationships

Global societies correspond to those concentrated areas we discerned in the uneven fabric of social reality. Starting off from this division, which has the great advantage of not being an arbitrary one, let us now consider the tangle of relationships within the global society. It concerns those relations that are established between two individuals who belong to the same society. These we shall call the *actors*.

We have already seen that relationships can exist between members of two societies. When we refer exclusively to those relations that bring together actors of the same society, we shall use the adjective *societal*. Amidst this vast collection of social relations, societal relations are only concerned with the internal relations of a global society.

Why do we exclude others? This is simply a question of method. In order to analyse, or even simply describe, the internal relations of a global society, one must find, or at least introduce, some kind of order. This will be facilitated if we neglect, for the time being, relationships which cross the boundaries of a society.

We also exclude from the field of societal – as well as social – relationships the relations between an individual and the physical world which surrounds him (relations of thought or action, fear or participation); between an individual and systems of ideas or forms (relations of fidelity and conversion, of conception and creation); between an individual and such entities as spirits and gods (relations of magic or religion, of cult or possession). Important fields of

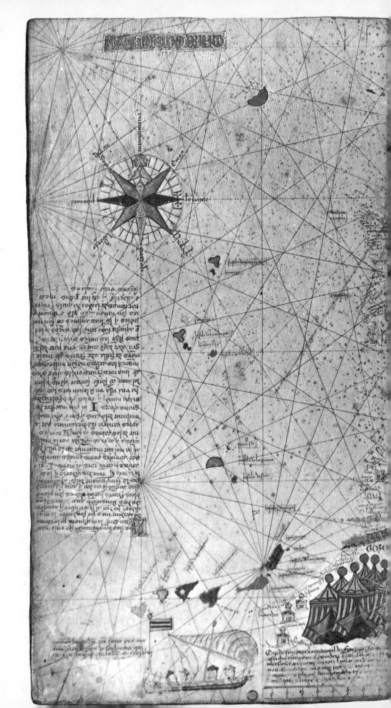

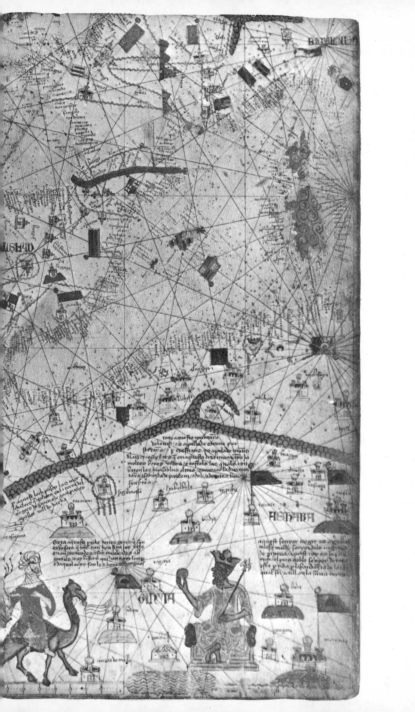

human activity do not fall within the scope of sociological analysis as such. Exclusion is the price of keenness of analysis.

Societal relations do not just happen haphazardly, they are not set up on the spur of the moment. When A wants to exchange goods with B, he approaches him in a different way from when he tries to arrange the alliance of two lineages by marrying the nephew of A to the niece of B. A does not have to invent these different ways of behaving. Like every other member of the society, he knows that an economic transaction occurs in a certain specified place, at a certain time of the day, and is introduced by certain standardised phrases, while a discussion about a proposed marriage will take place in an altogether different context. Nor will B be taken unawares. From the beginning he will know what is on hand, and if he does not want to accept A's commercial or matrimonial propositions, he will refuse, in the manner appropriate in either case, but not by improvisations. A will readily see which way the wind is blowing, and so need not be humiliated.

To a certain extent, societal relations unfold according to a preexisting schema. This schema can be an explicit norm (for example, matrimonial relationships require conjugal fidelity); but more often than not it is expressed by the modal behaviour (for example, in a certain society most married couples are faithful, thus the matrimonial relationship in this society incorporates fidelity within its schema). There can be a contradiction between the ideal behaviour or norm, and the usual behaviour or mode, (for example, the norm is fidelity, and the mode, adultery). In this case, anticipated ways of evading the norm will be established and provided for (the schema of adultery will make it necessary, for example, for the adultery to be clandestine but tacitly admitted by the husband or wife; for the partner to belong to the same social class, and not to have any material gain in mind, etc.) There exist rules even for breaking the rules.

Not all relationships between members of a society are schematised. If there is no precedent or no memory of one – which comes to the same thing – one has to be invented. Supposing two adults form a homosexual relationship in an isolated and restricted society, where such a thing has never been heard of before, the relationship established by these two people (we will not call them 'actors') will not follow any rules. It will be an interpersonal rather than a societal relationship.

Networks of societal relations

Seen from inside the society, multiple societal relationships do not seem to be just lumped together. They are perceived as having qualitative differences, and are immediately arranged in categories. A man distinguishes between relations with his chief and with his parents, relations with priests and with merchants, and so on. In addition, relationships in each category are seen to be tied to one another. One is tied, as if by a chain in which father and grandfather are the links, to the patriarchal lineage head by blood. One is tied to one's collaterals by descent from a common ancestor. One is tied to the king, all intermediary authorities, and all the other subjects of the same sovereign, by political relationships. Those born in the society in question immediately perceive both the classification of societal relations into several large categories, and their organisation within these categories. In fact, this perception is based on a more or less explicit social theory which the man in that society absorbs during childhood or youth, and which he does not generally have the chance to question.

The anthropologist's networks are made up of the same type of societal relations. These are organised, and so form configurations of relationships. But these networks as seen from the inside of society do not necessarily correspond to those that emerge from

Table 1   Models for ten elementary relations[1]

Seven institutionalised societal relations[2]

Elementary relation of:	Actors (A/B):	Roles of A/B:	Sanction:
Kinship	kin/kin (descended from same ancestor)	being solidary with B/ being solidary with A (general solidarity + specific rights & duties)	collective reproba- tion → excommunication
Alliance	affine/affine (allied through marriage)	supporting B/ supporting A	withdrawal of support → breaking of alliance
Government[3]	ruler/ subject	commanding B/ obeying A	coercion
Inequality and equality	superior/ inferior equal/equal	behaving according to A's rank respecting B's rank/ same for B	collective reproba- tion → loss of status
Feudality[4]	lord/vassal	defending B/serving A	penalties provided for in the covenant → termination of covenant
Association	associate/ associate[5]	co-operating with B in the pursuit of associa- tion's ends/ same for B	penalties provided for in the charter → ejection
Exchange of goods[6]	dealer/ dealer	giving goods and ser- vices to B for other goods and services provided by B/ same for B	payment of goods equivalent to the ones due and damage

Three non-formalised interpersonal relations[7]

Elementary relation of:	Actors (A/B):	Roles of A/B:	Sanction:
Power	dominant/ dominated	requiring a certain behaviour from B/ conforming to A's requirements	deprivation inflicted on B
Dependence	protector/ dependent	granting vital protection to B/ offering compensation to A	withdrawal of protection/ withdrawal of compensation
Reciprocity	giver/ counter- giver	giving a gift to B/ giving back a counter-gift to A	breaking of the relation

Notes:

[1] These relations are elementary in the sense that – in each one of the two categories – they are not reducible to one another.

[2] Each one of the seven relations is the focus of a specific societal network. The latter is separately institutionalised in each global society where it appears.

[3] Or political relation.

[4] In the clientship relation, the actors (patron/client) have roles similar to the lord/vassal ones but they are neither described, nor sanctioned in a covenant.

[5] The subsidiary relation associate/non-associate is based on the pressure the association can bring to bear on outsiders, and is not societally institutionalised.

[6] Or economic relation.

[7] These three relations are diffused. They are not separately institutionalised; they do not create around them societal networks but they may be conveyed by societal networks.

sociological analysis. In fact the first are based on the experience of only one society, and the function of the theory which is extracted from this experience is to justify, and consequently strengthen, the existing social order. The anthropologist's viewpoint, when he attempts to review these networks, is different. He employs concepts which can be applied to several societies, for any social science is comparative. He looks for simple criteria which enable him easily to identify like phenomena when he studies a new society in the field.

These two views of society, that of the participant and that of the outside observer, are not necessarily opposed in terms of true or false. They both have different ends, and both can be 'operational': the one provides members of the group with a satisfactory explanation of the workings of the society, and hence reinforces the social *status quo;* the other allows for the incorporation of new facts into anthropological knowledge, and perhaps a way of advancing the theory. We will here choose the second point of view.

Our classification of societal relations into networks is, moreover, very close to classifications which exist inside many African societies themselves. We have simply tried to use very ordinary concepts (such as politics, economics, etc.), not losing sight of their basic meaning, but at the same time linking them to simple criteria. Our aim is to be able, for example, to compare political networks in different global societies with the certainty that we can attach the same labels to the same situations. To say that a particular institution in Ankole is feudal (Ankole, during the traditional period, was a kingdom in the region of the Great Lakes) is to say that it basically resembles other so-called feudal institutions. From this it follows that one can compare these various feudalities, and generalise about them. It is important then to have a very clear idea of what one means by feudal relations. It is not enough to find certain analogies between the hereditary aristocracy of an African state and the aristocracy of medieval Europe to be able to conclude that one is dealing with a feudal society.

A small number of societal relations are not reducible to anything more basic. It is from these simple fundamental types that stem the many varied concrete relations which continually arise in a society. These relations, which derive from observed relations, are models, in the sense that concrete relations seem to conform to them. They are not ideal models, archetypes that exist *a priori* in the human mind, but abstract models of social reality. These we shall call models of elementary relations.

We can distinguish seven main elementary relational models in the social reality of African groups (see page 22). The elementary *political* relationship exists between two actors, the ruler and the subject. Their respective roles are to command and to obey, and this is sanctioned by the use of force. The relation of *social inequality* is found between two actors of superior and inferior status, whereas the relation of *equality* is found between two actors of the same status. The relationship of *dependence* unites a protector and a dependent on the basis of an agreement between the two actors (the feudal relationship is a variant of this). In an *economic* relationship, goods and/or services are exchanged between two actors, who, for want of a better word, we shall call dealers. *Kinship* relations link the descendents of a common ancestor, while those of *alliance* (affinity) bind together two actors in matrimony, either directly or through a group. Finally, the *association* relationship binds actors who voluntarily unite in order to reach a common goal.

In this introductory chapter, the enumeration of very succinct definitions is meant merely to point the way. These models can only be evaluated when one finally applies them to African sociological analysis.

Each of these seven models is specific of relations organised in a network. This does not mean that all political relations are simply of a coercive kind, but that, in one way or another, the mark of the political network is physical force. When one attempts to locate a relationship in a network, models can serve as criteria. In the same way rank is the distinguishing mark of social inequality. On the other hand, models of elementary relations are sufficiently different from the real cases from which they derive to make possible comparison of the realities they represent. Thus each model gives the network its internal unity, and differentiates it from others.

These seven elementary relations do not, of course, exhaust the vast fund of human relations in all their richness and variety. They are given a special place here because they create networks which, on the one hand, more or less correspond to the internal categories of each society, and, on the other, constitute guide-lines which are anthropologically useful. There are other relations which have a wider application, for our models are limited for the sake of precision. Thus the concept of inequality encompasses a greater number of relations than does our model of social inequality. Thus, the dependence of two lovers is not included in our societal network of dependence.

Power is one of those relations which does not give rise to a distinct network. Instead, it cuts across all of them. Relations of power exist in addition to those relations which exist between actors united by kinship (as, for instance, the lineage head and his grandson) dependence (as the lord and his vassal) or social inequality (as the aristocrat and the commoner). These power relations are in a way sustained or expressed by the network, but do not blend into it. Threads of power weave their complex patterns through the social fabric, criss-crossing from one network to another.

Why should one attempt to see the African social world from the point of view of power, *sub specie potestatis?* We do this in order to add another dimension to sociological analysis, and one that is absolutely essential.

In Africa, as elsewhere, power is a value of prime importance for the individual or the group – a universal value, for it gives access to the 'good things of life', and even, sometimes, to mere survival. How is power distributed in a society? How is it acquired? Its paths are often obscure for the very reason that power does not constitute a network of specific social relations; it utilises several channels. Members of a society who have power at their disposal hold it, and exercise it through several networks.

Power over nature is achieved by different techniques of production: hunting an antelope in the grassland; Nyamwezi men threshing sorghum in Tanzania, and textile production by craftsmen.

Power over nature, oneself and others

In the broadest, most fundamental sense, power is the capacity to produce desired effects. Attributed to a purposive being, this capacity can be exercised over nature. With techniques of production – agriculture, animal husbandry, handicrafts, industry, to cite only a few – man shows his power over his environment. From it he extracts all that is necessary to sustain and even advance his group. The domination of human societies over their physical environment grows as these techniques develop. Power over nature is primordial. A society can increase its population, diversify the activities of its members, and add to the complexity of its institutions, according to the quantity of goods it produces. Each great technical stage of development known to Africa – hunting and gathering, root-crop and cereal cultivation, pastoralism, handicraft, industry – defines a type of power over things, a certain capacity to produce the desired effects, and it creates a specific civilisation. So much for the importance of power over nature.

This study, however, is devoted to the analysis of the other kind of power – power over men. Since we are concerned with social relations (i.e. between individuals), we do not refer to talent, the ability of a person to produce desired effects by his own activity. The power that a writer has to create a work of art, or an athlete to perform a certain feat, is not a social relation; it is an ability to utilise innate gifts and acquired habits. This ability may serve as the seat of the power which may ultimately be exerted over others, but it is not in itself this power.

Sociologically perceived, power is an interpersonal relationship in which an actor obtains the desired behaviour from another actor. Let us call the first actor the dominant one (represented by D) and the second, the dominated (represented by d). Power is then the ability that D has to compel d to do what he (D) wants. The behaviour of d in this case, constitutes the 'desired effects' of the very general concept of power. This idea of the power relation is closer to the concept of Dahl than to that of Russell. According to Russell, if A and B have the same desires, and if A obtains all that B has obtained, and on top of that has been able to reap some extra benefits which B has not been able to do, A has more power than B[1]. Russell evidently approaches the power relation in a comparative and quantitative way. There is, in fact, no interaction between A and B. In Dahl's view, it is a question of relations between social units such that the behaviour of one or more units (the responsive units) depends in some circumstances on the behaviour of other units (the controlling units). He adds, furthermore, that the causal relationship bears a close resemblance to that of power[2].

This definition of the interpersonal relationship of power (D obtains the desired behaviour from d; or, according to Dahl's formula, the behaviour of the responsive unit depends on, or is caused by, the behaviour of the controlling unit) is a reasonable one, and must be mentioned at a certain stage of our research to establish clearly what is fundamental in the power relation: the capacity to obtain from another what one wants. But as it stands, it is not easy to use this concept in the kind of sociological analysis attempted here.

External criteria of power

The reason for the above is that we can only identify these power relations by the recognised techniques of anthropological or sociological research. There are fields in which only introspection would allow one, and even then with difficulty, to determine if there were a dominant and a dominated in a given relationship. A chief enjoys great prestige: this might be called a power relation if he both wanted this reputation and managed to persuade other people of his great and exemplary qualities. If, on the other hand, he gained renown without really wanting it or trying very hard for it, we are not entitled to analyse this phenomenon in terms of power. If a man wants to seduce a woman, and succeeds, we have a dominant and a dominated actor. If a man and a woman who are attracted to one another become lovers, there is no such power relation. It is impossible to venture into the maze of intentions and motivations without using the refined and lengthy techniques of psychology.

What then are the distinguishing marks of power relations as far as the anthropologist is concerned? The only directly observable criterion is that the dominant actor uses force to obtain the desired behaviour from the dominated. The king who commands obedience by coercion or the man who gains sexual access by rape are visible expressions of the power relation. But when methods other than those of physical force are used, one must have recourse to a criterion of interpretation. When an actor obtains goods and services from another actor without a return, this can be interpreted as a power relation. One assumes that a person does not willingly part with these things except in exchange for other economic values.

Without this hypothesis, we could never say that prestations in cash, kind, or work, owed by subjects to their sovereign, or by dependents to their lord, in any way demonstrated the power of rulers and protectors. These prestations would simply be the counterpart of the rulers' assurance of order, and the lords' guarantee of protection. The privileges of high position would not exist. But it is not easy to apply this seemingly indispensable hypothesis to traditional Africa. In many societies, the economic category is not clearly distinguishable from other categories: for example, when goods and services are used in a religious, familial or ceremonial context, they take on a different complexion from when they are used in the strictly economic sense. Economic equivalence is, moreover, difficult to establish in self-supporting systems where goods are produced and consumed by the same group without going through a market. Thus the necessity for anthropological guide-lines forces us to limit the scope of our definition of the interpersonal power relation. We must exclude interaction where the dominant actor tries to win non-economic values such as affection, prestige, admiration or glory, from others. We cannot learn by our normal methods whether pressure has been applied (apart, naturally, from force, which is observable but hardly conducive to winning a man love and renown). There remain those relationships in which a person can command goods and services from another without offering an economic equivalent in return.

The dominant actor's means of applying pressure

Max Weber defined power as the probability that an actor within a social relationship will be able to carry out his own will despite resistance[3]. Nothing could better emphasise the non-subjective and perhaps even measurable character of power (if it is a matter of probability, it can no doubt be calculated). Weber adds, however, that this is so 'regardless of the basis on which this probability rests'. Knowledge of these bases on which the probability of implementing one's will rests can be important for our anthropological analysis of power in social networks.

These bases are the means of applying pressure which enable one actor to play the dominant role in relationship to the other who becomes the dominated. Coercion, protection and pre-eminence are such means. A king can threaten his subjects with the use of force; a lord can withdraw his protection from his dependent; a man of superior status can humiliate his inferior. In all three cases, the dominant actor can obtain goods or services by virtue of the fact

A diviner belonging to the Hutu stratum
in Rwanda. He uses a tallow candle
and foresees future events according
to the direction of the flame.

that he can deprive the dominated of that upon which he depends. By political domination, he can deprive him of life, limb or freedom of movement; feudal domination can deprive him of his security, while the domination of a superior over an inferior can deprive the latter of his dignity. This aspect of deprivation is so fundamental that it even enables one to define the interpersonal power relation in a purely negative way: a relationship in which an individual can inflict a severe deprivation on another individual[4].

The efficacy of the means used to apply pressure obviously depends on the severity of the deprivation. Thus it is generally agreed that in the three cases mentioned above, loss of life is more severe than loss of security. Likewise, loss of security is more serious than loss of face. We can say, then, that political pressure is more efficacious than the pressure of inequality. This is 'common sense' to the western mind. Our judgment is based on the relative importance we accord these three values: life, security, and self-esteem. In other societies, this hierarchy of values might be different. We have to refer to an accepted hierarchy of values in any given society, or even segment of that society, in order to appreciate the relative efficacy of means of applying pressure. Thus in Rwanda a traditional kingdom in the Great Lakes region, the Tutsi section of the population, like many aristocracies, was chiefly concerned not to lose face. Many an edifying tale told to young Tutsi recounts the story of the nobleman who preferred death to dishonour[5]. It is a matter of cultural values that are held by a group and not of the exceptional opinions of some non-conformist. As such the latter are not the concern of the anthropologist.

The fact that the efficacy of pressure depends on cultural values sheds light on an essential aspect of the limitations of power; namely, the way the dominated man interprets the deprivation with which he is threatened. If he attaches no importance to that deprivation, the power the dominant man holds over him will

vanish. For the man who does not fear dangers and tribulations, the threat of withdrawal of his lord's protection brings no pressure to bear on him, and it will not force that man to do what the lord wants. In a society of men determined to suffer and die, coercion would be ineffective as a means of power. Fortunately for rulers, the will to live is a universal cultural value (no doubt because it is rooted in a biological constant). But other values of which an individual can be deprived are somewhat less universal. A relationship of power can only fully be established when the dominant and dominated share the same value system, or at least when the dominant conforms to the values of the dominated.

Means of applying pressure are not limited to the three types we have just mentioned. Any attachment to a value can furnish the means of pressure on someone to the person able to dispossess him. We shall see that, in most African societies, the value of the ancestor's benevolence is an important one. The man who can curse one of his descendents in the name of the ancestor has in his hands an effective means of applying pressure. A husband who is fond of his wife can be the object of pressure on her part, if the matrimonial organisation of the society makes it easy for her to return with her children to the arms of her family. The sorcerer who can cause disease though his knowledge of magic spells and secret rites, the healer who can restore health, the judge who can settle a case in favour of one of the defendants, all these possess the foundations of Max Weber's probability, the probability of obtaining what they want from individuals in spite of the latter's reluctance.

Restrictions in our study of power

It might be useful, at the end of this chapter which has tried to define the way we shall use the concept of power, and has explained our working hypothesis, to insist upon two limitations to such a study.

The interpersonal relation of power, in the widest sense, can be schematised in the following manner:

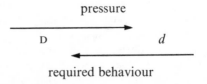

The dominant obtains the behaviour he requires from the dominated by means of the pressure he has brought to bear on him. This diagram can be applied to any kind of pressure and any kind of required behaviour. The mother who tells her child that she won't love him if he doesn't eat his soup, or a head of state who warns his parliament that he will resign if his prime minister's policy is not approved, or the man who tells a woman that he will commit suicide if she refuses to marry him, are all applying pressure. If they manage to procure the required behaviour, the power relation is complete, and corresponds to our schema. The fact that the parallel arrows point in opposite directions is not meant to suggest reciprocity. Properly speaking, there is no real exchange. The dominant one does not give anything, he threatens to take away. The arrow from d to D shows only that the dominant one has got his way. The behaviour required is not necessarily directly advantageous to him. Neither the mother nor the head of state profit themselves from the behaviour they take such pains to procure.

We will use a more restricted schema:

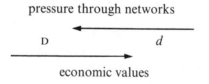

pressure through networks

D d

economic values

First, we consider only the pressures that are channelled or created by societal networks. The curse of the ancestor is communicated by the kinship network. But blackmail by suicide is not, to our knowledge, channelled by any African network. This first restriction eliminates therefore certain bases of power. Then – a second restriction of wider scope – we consider only those power relations where the required behaviour of the dominated individual is limited to prestations of goods and services normally obtained in exchange for other economic values. As indicated above, the only reason for excluding other forms of required behaviour is our inability to detect them by the acknowledged techniques of anthropological investigation.

In 1938 Bertrand Russell, in a book devoted to the subject, stated that power was the fundamental concept of the social sciences, corresponding to the concept of energy in the physical sciences[6]. We know that it is just an illusion to attempt to reduce diverse phenomena to a single principle. The miracle of key-concepts is usually a short-lived one. It is not our purpose to reduce all African social relations to relations of power, but to analyse networks as supports and mediators of power. We hope, thus, to treat African social reality in a new way.

3 Descent from the same ancestor

If we were to consider only the independent period – the third stage in African cultural evolution since the middle of the nineteenth century – we should not begin the examination of networks of societal relations with kinship. In the Africa of today, as in all societies moving into the era of industrial urbanisation, the functions which gave kinship its prime importance in agrarian and village societies seem to have been taken over by other networks. In the past, the newly married man would ask his kinsmen for a plot of the collective patrimony which he would then cultivate with his wife in order to provide for his new family. Today, a man's wages assume an ever-increasing importance in the upkeep of a family, even if he does not live in a town. Furthermore, he would not approach his kinsmen for employment – as a result of which, the kinship authorities are less able to exert pressure on him.

Nonetheless kinship networks, even in big African cities, still retain a strength which has long since disappeared in western Europe and north America. This strength can be explained by the very recent past, when groups of relatives, for the bulk of the peasant population (who, in fact, form more than eighty per cent of the black population in Africa south of the Sahara) constituted the most important social framework in the individual's life. This is further reinforced by the permanent value which modern Africa seems to accord to kinship (and, after all, industrial Japan also recognises the persistence of ancestor worship).

Common ancestry

Why were kinship systems of such great importance in traditional Africa? They were important because of the functions they fulfilled, and not because of the principles upon which they were based. We will nevertheless begin by recalling these principles, for the sake of clarity.

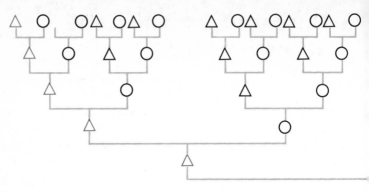

Figure 1

△ men   ⌐____⌐ indicates the relation of spouses
○ women   ⌐___⌐ indicates the relation of siblings

A and B in the diagram are brother and sister. All the other men and women shown are their biological ancestors. Their socially recognised ancestors are limited to men shown by a red triangle in a patrilineal society, and to women shown by a green circle in a matrilineal society.

Africans, like ourselves, do not recognise as ancestors all those who are biologically so (two parents, four grand-parents, eight great-grand-parents, etc.). They choose to recognise only one line: it can be either the paternal line (like ourselves) where ancestry is traced uniquely through the males (Ego's ancestors are his father, his father's father, the father's father's father, etc.), or the maternal line (Ego's ancestors, whether Ego is male or female, are thus the mother, mother's mother, etc.). The principle of descent adopted is often justified by theories of the relative importance of the masculine and feminine role in conception. Among the agricultural Yao (who today number about 400,000, spread through Malawi, Tanzania and Mozambique) it was thought that the embryo existed inside a woman's womb before any sexual union occurred, and that all that the sperm did was to awaken it. Looked at from that point of view, the child is almost exclusively the mother's creation, and this, for the Yao, reinforces matrilineal descent. On the other hand, for the Rwanda, who are patrilineal, the male plays a large part in conception. Sperm was not only necessary to start a foetus, but repeated contributions during pregnancy were needed for development.

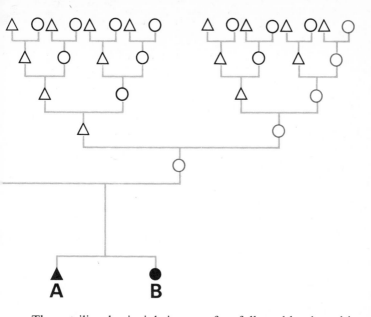

A   B

The patrilineal principle is very often followed by the cultivators of the Equatorial forest, who belong to what we have called the civilisation of the clearings, whereas descent through women is particularly found in what is known as the 'matrilineal belt' in the savanna region which extends south of the Equatorial forest at the 4th parallel south, west to east, crossing the whole continent, and approximately corresponds to the 'civilisation of the granaries'[1].

Whether ancestry is reckoned through one line or another, it cannot be traced back indefinitely from generation to generation, if it is used to define groups among the living. So that the line comes to an end with some ancestor who is famous because he led the group to some favourable spot where their descendants still live, or introduced a new species of plant which is still cultivated, or established an important social rule such as preferential marriage between cross-cousins, or for any other important action attributed to him. This ancestor is the reference point determining which actors belong to which kinship network among the members of a global society. All those men and women who can trace their ancestry back to the same ancestor, by either masculine ties (in a patrilineal society) or feminine ones (in a matrilineal society) are considered to be kin (or consanguineal relatives).

The kinship bond is not, as it has become in contemporary Europe, largely nominal. It creates a network of relations in which the actors have very well-defined roles. There is, firstly, the common role of all kinsmen towards all others; then there are specific roles according to the place one occupies in the network (older brother *vis-à-vis* younger brother, grandson *vis-à-vis* grandfather, etc.).

Up to now we have treated the tie of kinship as if in any given society, there were only two alternatives, to be kin or not kin. This was so in some traditional societies, but in others there were degrees of proximity in kinship. One can conclude from the many monographs written about African societies that three very distinct degrees of consanguinity were recognised in these societies: lineage, clan, and tribal kinship. These terms obviously belong to the vocabulary of anthropology, but the type of relations they designate correspond to distinctions also made in African terminologies. We are dealing, then, with concepts arrived at by induction.

Lineage relations unite all those who can trace back their ancestry to an actual common ancestor, naming the intermediate ancestor in each generation. *Clan relations* exist between descendants of a more distant, perhaps fictional, ancestor – an ancestor at least to whom one cannot trace back one's relationship through an unbroken chain of intermediate ancestors. Finally, *tribal relations* seem to be an extension of the kinship principle to all members of a global society. The unity of society is conceived as resting on common descent from one very distant ancestor, who belongs, furthermore, to a supernatural world rather than this one.

From the kinship point of view, tribal relations are interesting only because they draw attention to the place of consanguinity in the ideal systems of certain societies. It seemed to them so important that they could not conceive of any other basis of social solidarity.

Social density in a modern urban setting.
Dakar and the Cap Vert peninsula (Senegal).

Figure 2

This diagram illustrates a patrilineal descent system. All the living persons shown in red are patrilineal kin because they have their descent through males from the common ancestor A. The same applies to the living descendants of B, shown in gree Persons shown in black are not considered to be descendants of either A or B.

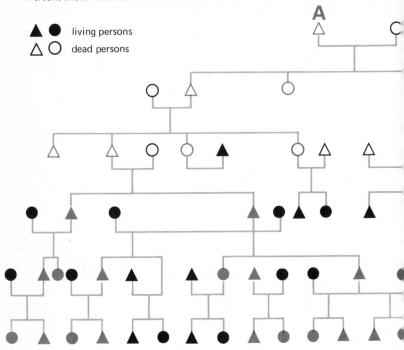

▲ ● living persons
△ ○ dead persons

Lineage and clan relations, then, are the two real constitutive elements of the kinship network.

Lineages and clans

When lineages and clans co-exist in the same society, they distinguish between themselves by characteristics other than the distance from an ancestor and the latter's reality. The relative proximity of the lineage ancestor – generally somewhere around six to ten generations – leads to the frequent appearance of new lineages which are formed by fission (supposing that the ninth generation of descendants from ancestor A, feel that there are too many living

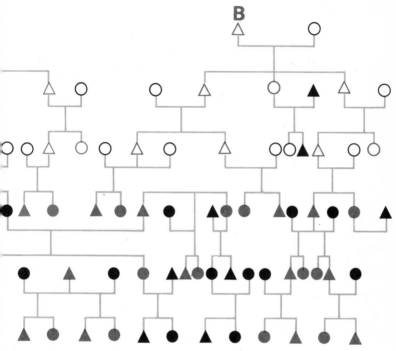

descendants in the line, they can decide to split up into two groups, one of whom will choose in the future to refer back to intermediate ancestor G of the fifth generation, and the other to intermediate ancestor E in the fourth generation.) The result is that the number of lineages in a given society is not constant. The number of clans of course is; the element of ambiguity in tracing back the generations makes it unnecessary for the clan to be redefined as time passes.

In actual fact these differences are not at all important, but they point to an observation: lineage and clan have two different functions. The first is an organised solidarity group (that is why it cannot expand too much without losing its efficacy) which has

common activities and a leading authority. The second also creates
solidarity, but of a less active kind. The clan is the shadow thrown
by the lineage, covering more ground, but with more blurred
contours, a less solid reality. All this leads one to the conclusion
that there is only one network of powerful relations of consanguinity
in a society, and this is the lineage.

Solidarity is the common role of kinsmen. Every individual
experiences the kinship network in a very direct way. In traditional
Africa, a man throughout his life, in the event of difficulty or crisis,
could always approach his lineage 'brothers' for help. He puts this
security to the test very early in life. The social horizon of a young
child includes his father's collaterals (who, in a patrilineal system,
often live very close to their common living ancestor) and he has
his meals with one or other of his relatives. Among matrilineal
peoples it is common for a boy, at the age of seven or eight, to go to
live with his maternal uncle (while his father's sister's children come
to live in the house where he was born). When the time comes for
him to marry, his relatives give him some assistance with the
bridewealth which he will give to the father (or maternal uncle) of
his intended bride. We have previously mentioned that his lineage
will put a plot of land at his disposal to enable him to provide for
his family. His lineage brothers will also furnish help, if he needs it,
to clear the ground, or in the event of a bad harvest, or when he
wants to build a new house. If he enters into litigation with a
stranger – even if he is found to be in the wrong – his lineage will
help him out of this uncomfortable predicament. Finally, if he dies
prematurely, he will not leave widows or orphans, in the sense that
both will be taken care of by his relatives.

In order to be in a position to offer this kind of security, the
'strong' kinship network (usually the lineage) is organised into
units, which both make decisions and carry them through. In the
preceding paragraphs we explained some of the advantages of

Kinship co-operation: lineage
brothers building a house in a
village in the Niger valley.

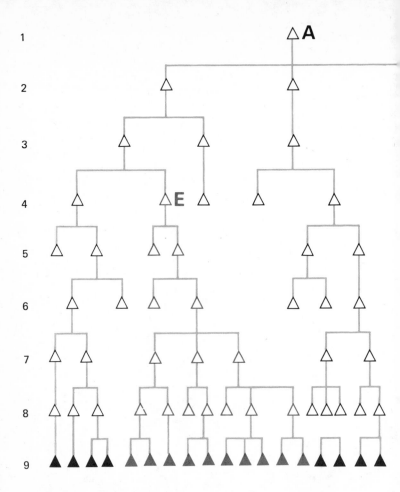

kinship solidarity for its beneficiaries. Its converse is the contribution (in work and goods, enduring risk and inconvenience) which the other relatives are frequently obliged to make. People may very readily agree to the idea of general reciprocity of services, but equally readily object, in Africa, as elsewhere, to have it applied to themselves ('I already helped x last week; why should I be chosen again to do another kinsman a favour today?'). There must be some guarantee that the tasks will be equally shared and imposed; the

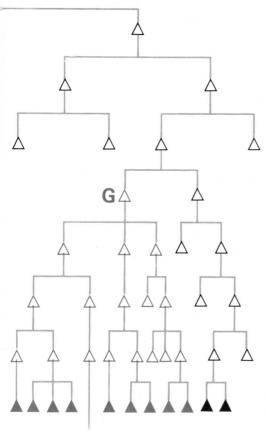

Figure 3

The patrilineal descendants of A formed a single lineage for eight generations. In the ninth, the descendants of E (fourth generation) and G (fifth generation) decided in future to call themselves the children of E and G, rather than of A. Thus two new lineages were created. But all the descendants of A to the ninth generation and beyond will continue to recognise their common ancestry and will form a clan.

lineage must provide mechanisms for the making and execution of decisions.

Lineage authorities

With an enthusiasm which owes more to nostalgia for a Golden Age than to any scientific judgment, anthropologists studying Africa have often dwelt upon the 'democratic' way decisions were

Wooden ram's head (osamasinmwi) from the Yoruba city of Owo. It was used on the ancestral altars of the chiefs of the royal lineage. Offerings were made each year in front of them at the time of the harvest. Rams symbolised the strength of the ancestors. (Lagos Museum).

collectively made in kinship groups. An assembly of all the fully adult males of the lineage (that is, married men and fathers) discussed questions which were of general interest. Each man spoke his piece, and at the end of a lengthy palaver, a consensus was reached, and a course of action adopted. Thus one could avoid the disadvantages of group decisions arrived at by majority vote: the minority's embarrassment (for they always stood to lose face to some extent), divisions within a group being made public, and thus aggravated, and the difficulty of persuading a minority to co-operate in the execution of something they had explicitly rejected.

This analysis is undoubtedly correct, but it credits African reality with a legalistic approach which is foreign to it. Everyone is certainly entitled to express his opinion, but one man's opinion may carry more weight than another's. The first reason for this is that a lineage is not made up of people standing in equal relationship to one another. In African philosophy, descent from a common ancestor is conceived as a vital link. He is the source of his descendants' strength and fertility, and this strength permeates all the intermediate links of the chain. The oldest living descendant of the ancestor is a necessary link in the life of the group, not only because he once begot children, but because he is still the channel through which the vitality of past generations of the lineage comes down to the present. He has the dreaded power of cursing, which means he can excommunicate from the lineage and cut off from the blood community those who are no longer worthy of belonging. On the level below the patriarch are the elders of the same and following generations (one of whom will soon succeed him) and they are listened to with all the respect accorded to individuals standing in such a close relationship to the ancestor. In addition, all the usual reasons why different individuals wield influence over a group come into play – competence, eloquence, wisdom, wealth, intelligence and experience – and have their usual consequence: some prevail, and the others follow.

Tshokwe wood carving of an ancestor.
(Tervuren Museum of Central Africa).

53

Decisions are made in a lineage in a non-authoritarian way (there is what could be called a preliminary public expression of opinion). But the end result is that these decisions represent the will of a very small number of people (perhaps only one) and these people are always the same ones in a lineage over a certain length of time.

How is a decision executed once it is reached? The patriarch can use ritual sanctions, but these are so serious that people are loath to use them (there is, in fact, only one, excommunication). What leads an individual to accept a lineage decision that affects him is religious fear, moral consciousness and, above all, collective reprobation. It is first the fear of the wrath of the ancestors, who can manifest themselves directly (without the intervention of the patriarchs) in the form of the punishments they send (illness, poor harvests, sterility). It is moral consciousness which, if decisions are not acted upon, can arouse painful guilt-feelings. It is collective reprobation which expresses itself in ridicule, more or less spiteful, or refusal to speak or answer when spoken to, and can lead to a breakdown of all co-operation, finally forcing a recalcitrant individual to leave.

Social reprobation is the most effective of all these different sanctions and even affects other sanctions (for example, an individual who is generally approved of by his relatives does not risk excommunication by the head, and does not suffer torturing remorse). Now lineage reprobation demands a unanimity of action which is more difficult to achieve than unanimity of decision. An influential man impresses the assembly, and gets the decision he wants. In ordinary everyday life, it is much more difficult for him to arouse collective reprobation, and without this, there is very little chance of executing a decision. The fact that execution implies a deep consensus of the whole lineage has to be born in mind by head, elders and other notables when they make decisions; and this, generally, tends to make the decisions more moderate.

Power from kinship

Properly speaking, these authorities (patriarch and elders) and notables (whose influence is largely based on qualities other than genealogical proximity to the ancestor) are the people who really control lineage affairs. Their importance is not determined by any one factor. This is plain to see in the case of the notables whose importance depends on individual achievement, and is often true of the other authorities. The patriarch is not necessarily the oldest man in the lineage. A patriarch chooses his successor, and age is only one of many criteria such as the ability to arbitrate disputes, influence in the assembly, and reputation outside of the lineage.

The kinship network is more fluid than the fixed principles of descent would have one believe. Those who aspire to a place of importance in the lineage, can win the necessary reputation and acquire useful support. Collective reprobation is a fundamental sanction; for the same reasons, collective approval is the determining factor for those who aspire to leadership in a kinship group (within the limits, naturally, of the principles laid down: however popular a young man may be, he cannot become lineage head).

Do lineage authorities and notables have a great deal of power? Do they have means at their disposal for applying pressure to obtain economic values without an economic return? This question is only valid if we put it in a sociological framework. Can the kinship network channel power relations? The security that a lineage gives an individual is so essential to his whole existence that anyone able to deprive him of it would have at his disposal a most effective means of applying pressure. The patriarch generally does have these means at his disposal, but the exercise of this sacred prerogative is, in fact, subject to the agreement of some of the other influential men of the lineage. This plurality of important persons guarantees, for all practical purposes, that at least one or other of them will oppose a somewhat arbitrary curse made against one of their relatives. Even if a patriarch succeeds in convincing all the other important people, it would still be necessary for public opinion to be won over. Otherwise the excommunicated man would meet with such sympathy from the group that the action taken against him would lose its edge.

On the other hand, if kinship makes mutual aid an obligation from which the elders draw considerable benefit, it does not give them a claim to regular dues. Nonetheless, the lineage authority who gives a young husband a field to cultivate can no doubt ask the young man to repay him with some other favour. The latter will find it hard to refuse for fear of not getting the particular piece of land he wants. In this case, the lineage head's power is of a very limited kind.

In itself, the kinship network hardly acts as a good vehicle of power relations. The application of pressure, feared though it is, is dependent on the support of group feeling. It is in this sense that African kinship groups can be called 'democratic'.

Kinship and politics

Politics and power are usually so closely allied that the above title may seem to be a repetition of the one in the preceding section. One can, in fact, define *politics* as the totality of means employed in the competition for important social roles in any network. It is the field of rival tensions in constant flux in which competitors manoeuvre to get to the top. As we have just seen, for the kinsmen who aspire to importance in the lineage the trump cards are popularity, reputation and wealth. In this book we have not used the term politics in this sense – convenient and legitimate as this is – in order to reserve it solely to refer to relations between rulers and subjects.

This instrumental notion of politics (the means of getting to the top) reveals its origin: that the summit *par excellence* to which political relations ought to lead is government. This is another reason for avoiding the use of this term to designate the strategy of access to a high position which does not give powers of coercion. For example, the patriarch stemming from some illustrious ancestor may enjoy an eminent position, but does not wield any real coercive powers, and his other means of applying pressure are very limited.

In the perspective of this study, *kinship and politics* denote an examination of relations which can exist between two networks of societal relations; namely, those between descendants of a common ancestor, and those between rulers and their subjects. We must first, however, consider a case which is common in traditional Africa, that of a society without any political network; that is to say, when the roles of ruler and subject do not exist, because no member of the society can use physical force against any other member.

It may seem surprising that any society can survive without a network of political relations. Would it not sink into anarchy and disorder? In his book *Political Anthropology*, Georges Balandier maintains that 'political power is inherent in *all* societies. It elicits respect for the rules upon which the society is founded; it protects society from its own imperfections, and in its own confines, it limits the effects of competition between individuals and groups'[2]. According to Balandier, political power is thus necessary because the social structure cannot maintain itself by custom and law alone. To support his views, Balandier quotes Lucy Mair who says in *Primitive Government* that 'there is no society where rules are automatically obeyed'[3]. Undoubtedly, Balandier's concept of political power is more all-embracing than our own (he defines it as 'resulting from the necessity of combating the entropy which threatens any society with disorder'.) He certainly adds that coercion is not the only one means of defence[4]. Nonetheless, the issue is on a quite precise question: is the sanction of physical force universal or not?

Traditional Africa contains so many societies in which one cannot observe any network of coercion that one cannot think of them merely as exceptions or marginal cases. Social rules are observed there as everywhere else, but not 'automatically'. They are respected because they go hand in hand with sanctions. Transgression of the rules has painful consequences for the offenders, and sometimes conformity is rewarded. But physical force, or the threat of it, does not figure at all in the range of sanctions. These *apolitical* societies are characteristic of the hunters' civilisation and of the agricultural civilisation of the clearings in the Equatorial rain forests and on the coast of the Gulf of Guinea. They exist in other places, too, notably among the herdsmen of the White Nile swamps.

In these societies, kinship networks fulfil conservative functions which elsewhere fall to the political networks. First, the resolution of conflicts internal to the society. Within the lineage, the authority accorded to the head and elders makes it possible to arbitrate disputes between kinsmen. Obviously an authority based on common descent is not available when the dispute is between members of different kin groups. What happens then? Lineage solidarity tends to extend the conflict, the 'brothers' of each adversary taking the part of their kinsman: this is the field of private vengeance or feud. But our worst fears are not justified: it does not degenerate into civil war with one faction seeking to destroy the other. Even when men come to blows they do not use the weapons commonly used against outsiders: this is because a a certain equivalence is recognised between damage sustained and the reparation sought; and also because – and this is most important of all – the heads of the two lineages involved make great efforts to effect a reconciliation. Basically, they want to continue to live together; not only do they speak the same language and share the same ideas on life, but they also exchange women through matrimonial alliance and goods on the economic circuit.

Control of land rights is another function we are used to seeing exercised by rulers. In the absence of the latter, this is dealt with by the kinship network. Clan territory constitutes a collective patrimony which is passed on from generation to generation, providing the descendants of that particular ancestor with the means of subsistence. It would be unthinkable to alienate this land. If it becomes necessary to enlarge the territory, there is no encroachment on the land of another group; new land is cleared. There has never been a shortage of land in traditional Africa; like water or air, it is an indispensable but free commodity.

Taking decisions in matters concerning the whole society has always been one of the functions of rulers, and one of the justifications of their privileges. Kinship networks also fulfil this function. In a global society, one lineage or clan generally has precedence over all the others: it may have been the first to arrive in an area, and been later joined by the others; or it may remember an ancestor further back than those of the other groups which were formed by fission from a common root represented by this very ancient ancestor. In this case, the patriarch of the first group will enjoy a certain pre-eminence over the rest. But he is not a chief; in meetings with heads and important people from other lineages, he will be the last to speak (which indicates that his opinion carries the most weight, since he brings the discussion to a close). Whether or not one has such primacy, affairs of general interest are dealt with at a meeting of the authorities of the different lineages, following the same procedure as that employed within an individual lineage. And some lineages wield greater influence than others for the same reasons that individuals do.

When these functions – resolution of conflict, enforcement of the rules of social life, decision-making in matters of general interest – are fulfilled by rulers, they are sanctioned by force. But this council of all the different lineage authorities only in fact possesses one sanction: collective reprobation. And how can this be effective when even in industrial societies, to take a familiar example, the important coercive powers of the police can only impose respect for law and order with difficulty?

Collective opinion only dissuades people from breaking the law when the society is small, and when it is impossible to leave it without running great risks. One should not be under any illusions about the term global society. A few villages, even a single one, a few hunting camps or a few bands of nomadic herdsmen constitute 'systems that are self sufficient in relation to their environment' according to Talcott Parsons' criterion[5]. Rudimentary techniques of subsistence do not call for the co-operation of many persons, and matrimonial circuits can only bring a few lineages into play (a lineage cannot constitute a global society because it is exogamous, and its members must find their mates outside; hence it is not self-sufficient). One consequence of the small size of a group is that all its members know one another personally; it is not possible to seek anonymity and thus avoid public censure. If an individual resists reprobation, it will only make things worse for him; the life of a stubborn offender can be made a misery, and if he persists in being obstinate, he has to decide to leave the society. But where does he go? He cannot live alone (even with the help of his elementary family if they accompany him). He has to be accepted by another society, which at best will make him feel like a tolerated outsider for a long time.

Collective reprobation worked because, under the conditions in which it was practised in Africa, it constituted a dreaded punishment.

Mutesa, the Kabaka of Buganda, surrounded
by his chiefs and courtiers. As the power of
the State increased, so the authority of the
patriarch and elders began to wane.

Chiefs and elders: opponents and collaborators

In traditional Africa, all societies have a kinship network, and most of them a political network too. Relations between these two spheres are often marked by a certain tension, latent or manifest.

Sir Henry Maine and Lewis H. Morgan, from their evolutionary point of view, thought that social organisations based on kinship belonged to an earlier stage in the development of human societies than did the emergence of political structures, which they identified with states. Anthropologists are no longer concerned with these vast problems of the origins of institutions and their hypothetical position in an evolutionary sequence. Interesting as they may be, such ambitious riddles cannot be solved today by our methods. But it is different when we are dealing with particular historical sequences whose development is fairly well known. A few of these special cases do exist in Africa; for them we can establish that a political organisation, a kingdom, for example, was preceded by a situation in which kinship groups alone exercised the key functions necessary to maintain the global society. The description in the preceding section holds true not only for certain societies at the end of the nineteenth century, but also for the known predecessors of some societies which possessed a political network at the end of the traditional period.

From this historical approach, the tension between the two networks, or more precisely between the actors who occupied leading positions in them, is easy to understand. As political relations developed, patriarchs and elders lost their control of affairs. The use of force appeared with the coming of a conqueror who imposed his authority by arms, or when an important man managed to form a group of devoted retainers who were ready to back him with force. Conflict was inevitable between this chief, whether he was of foreign or local origin, and the elders, since his powers could only

BOBO, CHIEF OF CHAGWÉ. MTESA, THE EMPEROR OF UGANDA. CHAMBARANGO, THE CHIEF.
POKINO, THE PRIME MINISTER.

grow at their expense of their authority. The chief always tried to oust important men from their positions in the administration of justice, the allotment of land, and general policy-making.

In the monarchies of the southern savannas and eastern high plateaux, where royal government was well established, tensions nevertheless continued until the end of the nineteenth century. Patriarchs held on to as much as they could of their old functions (certain hereditary offices, a kind of extra-terratoriality for the sacred places of the clan, and immunity from certain dues, all of which recalled their past autonomy) and when a weak king's reign gave them the opportunity, they tried to regain their old prerogatives.

Chiefs and kings, on the other hand, treated them with restraint. Rulers also belonged to lineages (one of the latter had become the ruling dynasty), and, like everyone else, were unable to conceive of a society without kinship networks. These close-knit groups, moreover, constituted forces which it would have been dangerous to neglect, and which could in any case be usefully employed in the administration. It was more convenient for rulers to claim dues from lineages than from individuals. For all these reasons, lineage authorities were associated in many cases with the rulers. Important elders formed part of the court, entered into ruling circles and reaped all the benefits of their political position. There was a sort of gliding from one network to another, from one apex to another. As we have seen, pre-eminence in a lineage gave a man very little power, but it was a means of entry into the ruling circles which did command considerable power.

Kinship in modern Africa

From the beginning of the colonial conquest political networks were either destroyed or subjugated. Since, at the end of the nineteenth century, the colonial set-up was essentially political, this could not be otherwise. Kinship networks continued to exist except in their societal functions. The colonial administration adopted the position of all rulers: its political prerogatives were to take control of the group, see that justice was done, enforce the law, and maintain order. These rights could only be exercised by the state or in its name. Lineages could now only deal with what the Europeans called private matters; but even in these fields their activities were tolerated rather than recognised. Western legal systems only recognise as subjects under the law individuals or groups to whom legal personality has been expressly ascribed. As lineages had never been endowed with a legal personality (as far as we know, none had ever requested it) they were legally non-existent.

Nonetheless, they continued to thrive as active solidarity groups. One could always count, in these new times as of old, on one's relatives. As the years of the colonial period went by, technical and

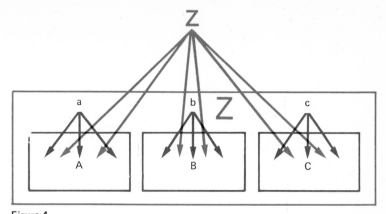

Figure 4
Kinship and government: two rival systems. Members of the lineages A, B and C are under the authority of their heads a, b and c, and are also subjects of the chief z.

economic innovations brought more and more marked changes in many aspects of African life: residence in the town instead of the village, a livelihood earned mainly from a cash income instead of by tilling the soil, an isolated life at the place of employment instead of the close contact with patriarch and kinsmen. Hard as it was under conditions which differed so much from those in which clan and lineage roles had gradually developed, people tried to stay faithful to the old ideas. The results were sometimes unexpected.

One outcome was that sociologists of the colonial period used to call somewhat disparagingly 'clan parasitism'. A young man leaves his village to seek work in the town; he finds it, and soon leads the life of a wage-earner; he rents a room, or lodging is provided for him by his employer; he buys the food and clothing he needs. One day, one of his relatives, also looking for work, comes to town. Kinship solidarity obliges the first man to extend a welcome to the second and offer him food and lodging until he has found work. Next it is his sister's son (in a matrilineal system) or his brother's son (in a patrilineal one) who comes to town because it has better schools. People visit to take advantage of the town's medical service, or out of curiosity aroused by its reputation. A man does not earn enough to cover all these extra expenses. He has to get an

The difficult transition from village to city
life: young men in Nairobi, and a Rhodesian
village depleted of young men, who are away
working in mining and industrial centres.

advance from his employer, a loan at high interest rates (lenders'
risks are high) or credit from the shopkeepers. This is the grim
picture that 'clan parasitism' conjures up. Colonial sociologists
sympathised with the poor young man full of initiative, victimised
by his clan 'brothers', but they tended to forget that he was also
the victim of an economic system solely oriented towards profit-
making.

Be that as it may, the solidarity of kinship ties was certainly
maintained during the colonial period, often unknown to the
Europeans who did not realise that there are very few things one
can refuse a descendant of the same ancestor. But until the last few
years of the colonial period, Africans were rarely in important
positions where they could wield any great power. Thus they could
only favour their kinsmen in relatively unimportant matters, at
least according to European criteria.

This does not hold true for the independent states, where
government and administration are, of course, exclusively in the
hands of nationals. African journalists and foreign observers often
denounce what they call 'tribalism', by which they understand
greater loyalty and attachment to traditional societies than to the
new states. This may be valid, but this loyalty to the little homeland
is mainly demonstrated by the preferential treatment that important
men accord to members of the same tribe or, more often, the same
lineage. This, moreover, is the reason why 'tribalism' acts as a
force of disintegration in young nation-states. Citizens from other
'tribes' are unable to identify with the new nation, which seems to
them to have been commandeered by a kinship group in the wider
sense of the term (we must remember that the traditional societies
known as tribes consider themselves to be all descended from one
ancestor), or in the strict sense (clan or lineage).

Today, in the Africa of the villages, where most Africans live,
kinship relations still constitute the essential network in an

individual's existence. In the Africa of the cities – particularly the capitals – blood ties still count for something in the competition for power. They are usually not indispensable, but they always provide useful short-cuts for those who want to get into positions from which they can set up profitable power relations for themselves.

4 Contracting an alliance

Descendants of the lineage ancestor are brothers and sisters, and they do not intermarry. If the solidarity group is to perpetuate itself, if the source of life coming from the ancestor is not to run dry, a contribution must come from outside the lineage. The foreign spouse, male or female, belongs, and to a great extent continues to belong, to another lineage. An alliance is formed between these two kinship groups.

A new family comes into being too. This family is of concern to the society as an economic, procreative and socialising unit (where children are brought up to become well-adapted members of their society). The global society is, in fact, dependent upon the family for both its physical and cultural survival. Consequently, in all African societies, marriage and the family form a network of societal relations between actors whose roles are meticulously defined.

Matrimonial alliances were very obviously of collective significance in traditional Africa from the point of view of the lineage and the global society. As several centuries of Western literature have dwelt almost entirely on the personal significance of marriage, and as the social organisations of the industrial age are no longer subject to the same traditional constraints, we are inclined to forget these collective aspects. Furthermore, in Africa, the contradictions which romantics too often see between the social and individual aspects of marriage, simply did not exist. The future spouses usually had a means, *de facto* or *de jure*, of making their preferences known. They could, moreover, almost always wreck a matrimonial project which was not to their liking. Finally, in small societies, choice was very limited, so that the choice made by the kinsmen and that of the future spouses coincided in practice.

It is hardly surprising that marriage alliances could be useful instruments in the power game. One only has to recollect the 'political' marriages of the royal and princely families in the Europe of the *Ancien Régime*, and the 'economic' marriages of more recent vintage between heirs to huge fortunes in land or industry.

Marriage, a tie between lineages

Whatever the principle of descent adopted – patrilineal or matrilineal – it is the woman who brings children into the world, and whatever the theory explaining conception, the processes involved in pregnancy and childbirth are slower, less frequent and more dangerous than impregnation. All nubile girls, because of their childbearing potential, are more valuable to the lineage than men.

This was especially so in the demographic conditions that prevailed during the traditional period. Life expectancy was very low, accidents in childbirth frequent, and infant mortality high. Besides which, endemic illness, epidemics and accidental deaths were a constant threat to the perpetuation and strength of the lineage. As the number of its members was always relatively small, only several concurrent misfortunes were needed to weaken it and prevent it from efficiently fulfilling its functions of security and mutual aid.

In a patrilineal system (and this is the most frequent in Africa) the effect of marriage was to transfer the potential fertility of a girl from her natal lineage to her husband's; any children she might bear would be descendents of her husband's ancestor, and not of her own; they would enrich another kinship network. From this point of view we can understand that lineages should concern themselves with marriage, and that the lineage which 'gave' the potential fertility of one of its girls to another lineage should try to make up for the loss. They could easily obtain this compensation if the lineage which had just received the girl in marriage gave a girl in return as a bride for one of the men of the first lineage. Marriage by exchange still existed at the end of the traditional period among

Traditional Kipsigi girls of marriageable age
had to go through the ritual of circumcision
before becoming acceptable as wives.

the hunters and some agricultural societies of the Equatorial forest. It seems to have existed throughout Africa before the traditional era, and it allows one to interpret correctly the meaning of bridewealth, which is a fundamental characteristic of African marriage up to the present day.

Marriage by exchange presents some problems. First, it means that at the moment when a man from lineage A asks to marry a girl from lineage B, a girl from A and a man from B must have the same intentions. Then, the two parallel marriages are interdependent, and if one were to end, it would be difficult to maintain the other. Finally, strict reciprocity limits the exchange to two lineages. Now, a union which is contracted by the presentation of bridewealth avoids the disadvantages of exchange. Bridewealth is not the purchase price of a woman, as was once thought, but a sort of credit in virtue of which the donor lineage can one day obtain another women from any lineage. We may cite two facts which support this interpretation. The goods transferred in a traditional society did not amount to anything much, they were not of any great economic value; they were simply the guarantee of a promise that would be honoured by any lineage. In some societies the bridewealth a person received remained distinct from his patrimony; its sole purpose was to enable him to obtain a bride for one of the lineage members at some future time.

Marriage has been defined as 'a union between a man and a woman such that children born to the woman are the recognised legitimate offspring of both partners'[1]. In Africa, it would be more apt to say that children are 'the legitimate descendants of the lineage who discharged the matrimonial debt'. It is not the consent of the two spouses, nor the decision of an authority, that constitutes marriage, but the transfer of lineage rights over the offspring. This transfer is effected solely by the remittance of bridewealth. In some societies this is made in several payments, the last coming only

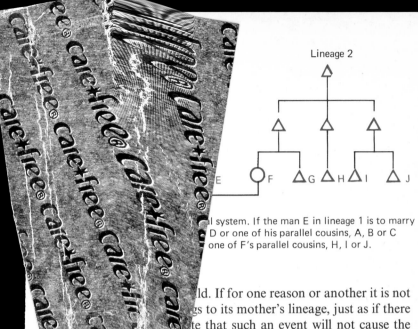

Lineage 2

...l system. If the man E in lineage 1 is to marry
...D or one of his parallel cousins, A, B or C
...one of F's parallel cousins, H, I or J.

...ld. If for one reason or another it is not
...gs to its mother's lineage, just as if there
...te that such an event will not cause the
...moral discomfort; the woman's own
lineage will welcome the new member and mother with open arms.
If a sterile marriage ends when all the bridewealth has been regularly paid, the latter must be returned to the lineage which provided it.

The organisation of African marriage clearly shows that it is,
above all, a union of lineages through the mediation of a union
between individuals. Thus the function of exogamy which Claude
Lévi-Strauss so clearly brought to light in *Les structures élémentaires de la parenté* (1949) is fulfilled. This function is to establish
communication in the form of women and goods between lineages
which without it would risk becoming closed and even hostile
sections of a global society, within which co-operation would be
risky.

Marriage and power

Marriage, for the spouses, is an alliance which creates a new family.
Is this institution, which promises its partners economic security,
sexual gratification and the possibility of bringing up their children,
also a vehicle of interpersonal power relations in Africa? Do certain

familial roles allow one actor to dominate another and obtain things of economic value for him?

The classic cliché which was very widespread among colonial Europeans was of a group of men sitting in the shade of the village square, smoking and chatting, while their wives worked in the fields, baby slung across their backs in a cloth. Like all clichés, it is an exaggerated and somewhat spiteful expression of not altogether imaginary facts. In many traditional societies the men, collectively in lineages or villages, set about the heavy work of preparing the fields – they did the clearing, the initial ploughing, harvesting and storing. But the women concerned themselves with the daily routine monotonous tasks. Their husbands would sometimes help them. Among African peasants a bachelor was at a disadvantage as a producer. Celibacy was considered as a misfortune and an anomaly mainly because it deprived a man of descendants and so broke the continuity of the generations, but also because an unmarried man had no one to cultivate his field and prepare his meals. An unmarried girl helped her mother in the fields and in the house.

It is true that, nearly everywhere in the world, the family is a unit of economic co-operation, and Africa is no exception. But everyone did not make an equal contribution within this unit; for instance, the wife devoted considerably more time than her husband to agricultural work. This difference is particularly significant in view of the fact that during the traditional period, production depended solely on work, since land, not being privately owned, was plentiful and free. A relationship of domination appears in the African family, parallel and, to some extent, based on the husband-wife relationship. A wife could resist and refuse to do certain things, and if she did this for long enough, she was finally led to leave her husband and return to her own family. This would deprive her of the companionship of husband and children and expose her to the

A groom and his kinsmen on the way
to his marriage ceremony in Zululand.

condemnation of the lineage. The latter would be very displeased at such a rupture, since it would deal a fatal blow to the goodwill existing between the two lineages.

The schema proposed on page 37 for the power relation in the strict sense is also valid in the analysis of the social microcosm of the elementary family (husband, wife and children). It also allows one to analyse the slightly more complex situation existing in the polygynous family: that is, in which a husband has several wives. Polygynous marriage was permitted in all traditional African societies, and indeed was the preferred form of matrimony. This was precisely because it gave a man a better chance than did monogamy of obtaining what he wanted of marriage: namely offspring and prosperity. Among peasants, the polygynous family was generally composed of two or three elementary families living in close juxtaposition. Each wife lived with her children in her own house and cultivated the field assigned to her by her husband. There is a direct relation between number of wives and agricultural production; the villager with two wives had twice as many consumer goods at his disposal as the monogamous man; the man who had three wives, three times as many, etc. Every marriage gave a man the opportunity of acquiring economic values without an economic return, and every plural marriage increased his power.

Even in a matrilineal system the marital role confers the same kind of power over the wife. Descent through the female (matrilineality) does not mean government by women (matriarchy), nor even that women are dominant in the family. The wife's matrilineal lineage is not represented by the woman herself, but by her brother; the latter does not exercise his authority over his sister's husband, but over his sister's children. There is no direct conflict between the roles of husband and brother-in-law, whereas there is this conflict between the roles of father and maternal uncle. It exists in relationship to a man's children who, because they belong to their mother's lineage, are under their uncle's authority, and the father normally finds it hard to accept this fact.

In the patrilineal family, where these tensions do not exist, the paternal role is also associated with a power relation *vis-à-vis* the children. Sons, at a very early age, will do various jobs for their fathers, and daughters will work in the fields. Later, by their marriages, arranged by the lineage, they give their father a potential means of applying pressure – that is to say, a winning hand in the power game he is playing, both inside and outside his lineage.

Marriage alliance and politics

A marriage alliance creates relations of political significance besides the power relations which exist inside a family between a father and his children, and between the very close allies, husband and wife. The rulers of traditional Africa were deeply involved in the lineage system. Their political predominance, even when it arose from foreign conquest, most often expressed itself in terms

Below A Ganda wife working in her husband's sweet potato field.
Left Wooden figure from the Tshowe tribe in Congo-Kinshasa showing a woman pounding cassava in a mortar.

of kinship. This was because kinship was so basic to African life, because it gave a sort of legitimacy to any power that was based on it, and because in practice close relatives and important members of the sovereign's family were members of the court, and had a certain share in the privileges of political power. This close association between the sovereign and his lineage was apt to arouse the envy of other kinship groups, who considered themselves just as ancient and illustrious as the royal lineage.

This potential hostility on the part of other lineages was one of the two major sources of anxiety to monarchs. They were hardly ever threatened by revolt from the inside (that is, by violent collective action in which one stratum of the population opposed the rulers) and even less by revolutions (an abrupt attempt to change the social order). Known traditions mention few events that could be interpreted as revolt or revolution, but they do mention what we would call *coups d'état*, that is, the seizure of the principal government positions by force. These *coups d'état* were attempted either by the monarch's close relatives (for example, one of his brothers who had been a possible choice to succeed the preceding king) or by rival lineages. The king defended himself against pretenders from his own lineage by preventive measures such as banishment or assassination; against potential manoeuvres by rival lineages, the king preserved and consolidated his political power by strategic marriage alliances. By taking a wife from each of the important rival lineages, the sovereign enlisted support, or at least neutrality. For his choice brought honour to the group the wife came from, allowing the lineage head and elders to reap some benefits from their new alliance, even to hope that the next king might be a son of their lineage. Political marriage alliances were largely practised by the European dynasties, but monogamy limited their strategic possibilities.

On a lower level than the political power game, marriage

alliances played an analogous role in relations between ordinary lineages. By refusing, under various polite pretexts, a request for the hand of a certain girl, or by delaying his answer, a man could exert pressure on the proposing lineage, and thus obtain favours from them. Or on the other hand, by establishing several marriage ties between themselves, the authorities of two lineages could form a sort of coalition which would then give them more influence in decision-making at village meetings.

The network of alliance relations (or *affinal* relations as they are sometimes called) is an indispensable complement to the kinship network. As descendants of the same ancestor cannot marry each other, they have to ally themselves to descendants of another ancestor. Alliance relations are better channels of power relations even than kinship. Thus kinship and alliance together are very instrumental in the political network.

Marriage alliance in modern Africa

The basis of alliance relations, polygynous marriage, contracted by the payment of bridewealth, survived both the condemnation of Christian missionaries during the colonial period and the more or less marked disapproval of the European administrations. It resisted these pressures very strongly; polygyny has always been very widespread (though it has never been practised by every single man in a society because the approximately equal number of boys and girls born makes this impossible). Civil or Christian marriages are accompanied by a transfer of bridewealth, and purely traditional unions are still very common in villages. But the typically African characteristics of marriage are modified by the urban conditions prevailing in an Africa which is on the threshold of industrialisation.

In the towns, individuals are separated from the organised body of their relatives; lineages were left behind in the often faraway villages. When a man and woman want to marry, the woman's lineage is represented by only one relative, often a very distant one; and it is to him that the bridewealth will go. The latter is no longer a matter of hoes, or cattle; in the monetary economy of the town it consists of cash. The woman's relative who happens to represent her lineage probably keeps the money for himself, and only thinks of making a profit. The bridewealth has been degraded into a purchase price which is haggled over, and has largely lost its original meaning, which was to guarantee to the wife-giving lineage the possibility of later obtaining another potential child-bearer. Urban conditions lead to individual-type marriage where payment of bridewealth seems like an antiquated relic of agrarian Africa.

Polygyny seems to be incompatible with urban conditions. A fixed income does not provide the means to support more than one household. Yet new circumstances, unforeseen by European sociologists, have made plural marriage possible in modern life. Largely by trading, women in the cities gain enough money to assure them economic independence. This makes polygyny economically feasible. Indeed there may be a movement towards units stabilised around the mother and her children (matrifocal), the marital role thus becoming secondary and even temporary. Up to now, these cases have been more conspicuous than numerous. Nonetheless, they are sociologically important in that they offer an original re-interpretation of a traditional institution which enables it to be integrated into modern African life[2].

In rural Africa, matrimonial and familial relations still carry great weight. The wife brings her husband's fields into production. If he spends a long time in employment away from the village, his wife has to work even harder than in the past. But when he returns, she is rewarded by the consumer goods he has bought. Alliances between lineages continue to be made, but the stakes are not so high, since the villagers are no longer ruled by an assembly of elders and notables but by an appointed official, an elected mayor or secretary of the local branch of the party.

In the towns, the husband is no longer in a position to exert strong pressure on his wife to make her work for him. Even in less exceptional cases than the ones we have just cited, it is generally recognised that a wife has the right to benefit from the profits her own activities bring. As far as the use of marriage relations in modern political competition is concerned, it is analogous to the use of kinship relations, but less efficacious. It is better to be a ruler's kinsman than his affine. But one has to be born a kinsman, whereas one can become an affine.

5 Government

In a book dealing with African societies from the point of view of power relations, one would expect the chapter on political networks to be of prime importance. Politics and power are so closely linked, not only in anthropological terminology but in ordinary usage, that the two terms have become practically synonymous. A country's leaders are indifferently termed 'the government' or 'the party in power', and the political system is often defined as the totality of power relations in a society. It is true that political scientists distinguish in theory between *power* and *political power*, but in practice they often neglect to differentiate them, or rather they seem to consider non-political power as a vague residual category not worthy of their attention.

From our point of view, this chapter is also of prime importance. For one thing, the political relation, sanctioned by particularly effective means, namely physical force, is clearly capable of supporting relations of power. It is also important because we believe that a clear anthropological analysis must not confuse power relations with political relations. This chapter is the place to attempt such an analysis.

Elementary political relations

Our point of departure for this network of societal relations is, as with other networks, an elementary relational model, *a posteriori* in the sense that it is an abstraction from observed relations. In most societies, indeed, one sees that some members order others to do or not to do certain things. When the latter do not obey orders, the former take coercive measures against them.

This 'command-sanctioned-by-constraint' relation recurs frequently between the same actors, and at one time or another every member of the total society is involved in such a relationship, whether in the role of giving the order or obeying it. These roles are, moreover, quite well-defined in every society: a man knows the kind of orders that will be given and received and the kind of sanctions that will be applied. This relationship thus seems to generate a stable organised network.

This is a brief resumé of the facts an anthropologist can observe in many societies. From subsequent analysis he can conclude that this controlling relationship of a network cannot be reduced to the various other relations which also occupy a central place in systems of relations. The anthropologist is acknowledging their comparative value when he states that this abstractly expressed relation is found in societies which are widely distributed in time and space. Finally our imaginary anthropologist decides to call the relation and the network 'political', the actor giving the order 'ruler', and the one who was to obey 'subject'. This is because of the similarity between the network born of the command/obey relationship and the network we commonly call a country's political organisation.

This brief summary, devised *a posteriori*, of a process which naturally was a much longer and indirect one in practice, both illustrates the method followed in this study, and anticipates certain objections to it.

One such objection, raised by Georges Balandier[1], emphasises the meagre content of political relations when one attempts to isolate them by an analytical process. We are not trying to deny the poverty of our definition. It is precisely because it incorporates so few elements that it is operational for purposes of identification and comparison. The anthropologist engaged in field-work needs simple criteria to enable him to distinguish, in the multiplicity of apparently unordered relationships in a community unfamiliar to him, those which belong to the network that he is concerned with. The comparative anthropologist (and all anthropological research necessarily has a comparative stage) must make sure that the category of phenomena he plans to study in different societies is defined the same way. Our concept of politics is, moreover, not doomed to remain in this skeletal form. At the end of the study of the political network of a particular society, or by comparing several such networks, we shall know the internal organisation of the group of rulers, the way they acquire their positions, the collective representations concerning chiefs and kings, the function of the political network, etc.

A number of Africanist anthropologists have started, instead of finishing, with the functions of the political system, since they define it by its functions. Radcliffe-Brown, in his preface to *African Political Systems*, a collection of eight short monographs which inaugurated the study of political anthropology in traditional Africa, states that 'the political organisation of a society is that aspect of the total organisation which is concerned with the control and regulation of the use of physical force'[2].

Nearly twenty years later, John Middleton and David Tait redefined political relations in terms of their function, that is, to assure social order[3]. Other Africanists found the maintenance of social order too narrow a notion, and preferred to speak of 'the maintenance of internal co-operation and external independence'[4], or even more widely as 'the need to fight against the entropy which . . . threatens to throw [any society] into disorder'[5]. In all these quotations, the political system is defined in terms of what it does: by its function.

One of the most important tasks of anthropology undoubtedly is to determine the function or functions of the political network. But *defining* a network in terms of function can lead to serious errors. It soon becomes apparent that a function (such as the preservation of social order, for example) is fulfilled by several institutions at the same time (state, church, synagogue, or economic system for example) but not always by the same institutions. Inversely, a given network (kinship, for example) fulfils different functions which vary according to the society and the period (administration of justice, regulation of marriage and land allocation, for example). A definition in terms of function would make identification and comparison almost impossible.

Territoriality and legitimacy are two elements frequently taken up in definitions of political networks. They do not seem to us to be essential. When rulers exercise authority over a given territory this facilitates the application of force; to make a person submit to force, one must first lay hands on him, which is most easily done if one has permanent control over the territory in which he lives. But this is not absolutely indispensable; for example the chief of a band of nomadic warriors, the captain of a battleship at sea, a guerilla leader in a country nominally under the rule of another government, can all create temporary political relations.

Legitimacy seems to us to be a secondary phenomenon on the level of the collective representations that a society projects of itself. Every society using its past and present experience of government has worked out a theory which justifies the existing government by hereditary rights or divine consecration, constitution or charisma, elections or plebiscite. Such a variety of principles of legitimacy well demonstrates the derivative character of the concept. If one attempts to define legitimacy in terms of the general consent of the governed, one does reach a more basic psychological reality; but how does one discover this consent? Can one say that the rulers of the African colonies met with the approval of their subjects? If the answer is no, can one then say that there was no government during the colonial period? Legitimacy, even when understood as consensus, cannot be usefully incorporated into the definition of political relations.

Political competition and relations between governments

The ruler-subject relation is the basic tie found in all the numerous interactions between members of a society. These interactions can appear very different and at times be misleading. A judge, who imposes the prescribed punishment in a criminal case on the guilty man, or makes the defendant pay damages in a civil one, stands in a political relation towards those he sentences because his decision can be implemented by force if necessary. For the same reason, tax-collectors and tax-payers, legislators and people submitting to the law, policemen and ordinary passers-by, all relate to one another in a way which, in the final analysis, is political. To be sure, the character of the ruler can be very blurred in certain roles, and his resort to force very indirect. But the presence of these elements (ruler and force) is enough to make a relationship political.

It is this political aspect of relations, different in other respects, that integrates them in a network which is organised and, particularly in industrial societies, very complex. We are concerned with a unified network, perceived as such. In calling for the separation of the state's three functions (legislative, executive and judiciary) the classic theory confirms that they are commonly combined. Furthermore, this is the norm in the monarchies of traditional Africa.

It is on the basis of these considerations that we distinguish the governmental network from other societal relations, and to it alone apply the term political. Is this perhaps too narrow a concept? If we limit the political field to relationships between rulers and subjects that are potentially sanctioned by force, do we not thereby exclude the struggle for power and international relations, two very important areas usually considered political?

The study of a network always entails an examination of ways of attaining the different roles. It is obviously more difficult to 'become a ruler' than it is to 'become a husband' or to 'become a

Monumental lion in a public square in Addis-Ababa. It symbolises the monarchical authority of the present dynasty.

father'. The competition is greater, and it has resulted on the one hand in the elaboration of institutionalised means of recruitment (co-optation, elections, competition, etc.) and on the other to all kinds of processes intended to ensure the success of the enterprise (well chosen marriage alliances, the favour of important people, corruption, etc.). The importance of the issues at stake, and the scope of the manoeuvres, have led students of government to develop this topic to a considerable extent. Our definition of political relations does not exclude it, on the contrary.

The relations between global societies which today are nations has always been a matter for the governments concerned. It is they who conduct diplomacy and war. These can be called political by a sort of extension of the term. If conquest succeeds, moreover, it generally leads to the inclusion of all the members of the defeated society in the political network of the winning side; they become subjects of the conquering rulers. As we intend to deal only with societal relations, that is those relations which unite all the members of a global society, we will not extend the political domain to diplomacy and war.

Monarchs and subjects

In traditional Africa, government was always monarchical. There was a chief or king at the head of every political network. Where the number of subjects and density of population allowed the monarch to rule directly, we call the political unit a chiefdom. It is called a kingdom when the sovereign has to delegate his power to officials who exercise it in his name. Among well-known examples we can cite the chiefdoms of the Bamileke (in the present Cameroon), the Bemba (Zambia), the Kikuyu (Kenya), the Lulua (Congo-Kinshasa), the Mbundu (Angola), the Serere (Senegal), the Tiv (Nigeria), the Yao (Malawi, Mozambique, Tanzania). This list,

which could easily be added to, shows that chiefdoms were very widely distributed in Black Africa. The same is true of kingdoms; we may mention the Ashanti (Ghana), the Bamum (Cameroon), the Fon (Dahomey), the Ganda (Uganda), the Kongo (Congo-Brazzaville, Congo-Kinshasa, Angola), the Lozi (Zambia), the Malinke (Senegal, Mali, Guinea, Ivory Coast), the Mossi (Upper Volta), the Rundi (Burundi) and the Zulu (Republic of South Africa).

In the monarchies, these 'one-man-governments', the chief or king alone had supreme command, but he was not the only ruler. There was always a group of associates around him who shared, to a greater or lesser degree, the responsibilities and rewards of his role. This group of rulers was heterogeneous; it included, in the

Carved wooden insignia which symbolise
the authority of the Yoruba chiefs.
(Museum of Lagos, Nigeria).

93

case of a kingdom, important relatives of the monarch, authorities from other lineages, counsellors in whom the king trusted, specialists such as diviners and healers, military chiefs and representatives from distant regions. This group, who naturally resided close to the monarch, accompanying him on his travels, constituted a court which fulfilled the functions of a central government.

In the kingdoms, some of which covered considerable territory, the sovereign's delegates made up a machinery of administration which was sometimes very complicated (as in Dahomey and Rwanda). Finally, wherever there was a political network, the execution of important orders was guaranteed in the last analysis by agents of force; from the simple bands of armed retainers of the Bemba chiefdoms to the regiments of the Zulu kingdom.

Monarch and court, administrative and executive agents, were rulers in the sense that their decisions, even when executed by subordinates, were sanctioned by actual or potential recourse to force. All the other members of the same society were assigned the role of subject in political relationships. Thus African societies were distinguished by a major division between rulers and ruled.

The roles of these two categories of actors were culturally determined in each society. Numerous monographs bear witness to this fact. We can only hope to show here the common elements in these roles in traditional Black Africa.

We have just seen that the group of rulers was quite heterogeneous. It was hierarchical: the power of some rulers extended throughout the kingdom, while that of others was limited to a district; a few made the decisions, and many executed them. It was a specialised group, comprising among others judges and tax-collectors, warriors and magicians. It was often split into factions fighting to promote their own interests. But all the rulers had a general role to fulfil in relation to their subjects. Without pausing over the finer points, let us consider this general role.

When a problem concerning the whole society arose, it was for the rulers to solve it. This might be something unforeseen such as an epidemic, an exceptional drought, or the approach of foreigners; or it could be one of those recurring events which gave collective life its characteristic rhythm, such as planting and harvesting, the initiation of an age set, or some seasonal ritual.

Judging was one of the prerogatives of every political authority; as was punishing delinquent law-breakers, and arbitrating disputes between two members of the society. One judged according to custom as it was expressed in precedents, rather than by injunction or general prohibition. The judicial function was not separated from the general role of ruler. Sometimes a king or important chief would delegate the task to a special judge, but the latter had no autonomy in its exercise; his judgments could always be amended by the political authority to which he was subordinate.

It was also part of the ruler's general responsibility to collect consumer goods and services. According to the type of production of different regions and the needs of the rulers, agricultural and pastoral products, meat and skins from hunting, fixed tasks (such as the construction or maintenance of the chief's residence), and days of labour, were exacted at regular intervals and whenever the authorities demanded it.

From the tenth to the nineteenth centuries, the city-states of the scrub zone (the Sahel) south of the Sahara and of the neighbouring Sudanese savanna were important centres of international trade. Caravan routes linked them to towns on the African coast of the Mediterranean. The products they exported were all precious goods: spices, rare woods, worked leather, ostrich feathers, and above all gold. In exchange the caravans brought salt, arms, cloth and copper. The rulers deducted as taxes a certain proportion of these imports and exports; they sometimes managed to take over entirely the exploitation of some natural resource. An Arab chronicler, El Bekri, in a text of 1067, mentions that all the gold nuggets found in mines in Ghana belong to the king; only the gold dust was left to the gold-washers.

The concentration of economic values is an essential element of the general role of rulers, whether in agrarian chiefdoms where villagers take a few baskets of millet and sorghum to their modest king, or in wealthy states raising taxes on precious goods. Without this constant influx of goods, how could the whole apparatus of coercion, the basis of the political network, be maintained? Force, the sanction of rulers, implies that a chief is in a position to feed at least the few men who at need can see that his orders are carried out. In the large kingdoms with their complex organisation, the subjects ensure for the king, court, officials and soldiers a standard of living generally higher than their own; so that these government personnel are not themselves concerned in the production of goods.

One must remember that pre-industrial Black Africa relied almost entirely on agriculture for subsistence. The raising of stock, which was essential to the cultural value system of the pastoral peoples, produced a very limited supply of milk and meat. Hunting was only a marginal activity. The returns from traditional agriculture were mediocre. African soils, except in the valleys, were poor, and vast areas such as the tropical forest were unhealthy for man; cultivation techniques were rudimentary. Under these conditions, levies of foodstuffs which would be insignificant in an industrial context had a high economic value.

Government and goods

Coercion is a luxury which not all societies can afford. When every member of the community has to devote all his time and energy to producing food which he and his dependents will then entirely consume, there is no one to specialise in coercion. First one has to

Golden jewellery which was made for the king of Ashanti, the Ashantehene. The top right-hand ring symbolises a serval 'which though neither leopard nor lion will not spare its prey'. The ring with an elephant signifies the omnipotence of the wearer. In strong and centralised kingdoms, most of the wealth was concentrated in the hands of the supreme ruler.

Altars at the ancestral shrine in
the Oba's palace at Benin, where
the Oba offers to his predecessors.

Joseph Munongo, chief of the Yeke, Congo-Kinshasa (*c*. 1958). The leopard skin at his feet, the shells of his headdress and his white tunic are symbols of his authority. These ritual insignia were created by the Chief Msiri who, in the latter part of the nineteenth century, conquered the present territory of the tribe and organised the Yeke political institutions. The pendant hanging from the chief's neck is a Belgian standard medal granted to chiefs recognised by the colonial authorities.

eat. That is why there is no political network in the hunting camps and the villages of the equatorial forest. Two conditions are necessary for the emergence of a chiefdom or kingdom: first, all the families, or at least most of them, must produce more than they consume; secondly, all or at least the greater part, of this surplus, must be concentrated in the hands of one man. For this single reason he is chief or king.

What does he do with the collective surplus at his disposal? He and his family eat well. Corpulence is one of the marks of political power. This is why, contrary to what happens in our consumer societies, it is respected and admired. Next he maintains his agents of administration and coercion. Finally he goes on to what Karl Polanyi has called redistribution[6]. The husked and dried grains and vegetables which have been brought to the chief are stored in granaries. Some of these provisions will be used for great communal feasts at seasonal rites; the rest will be kept for the sustenance of the group in the event of famine, or for the hungry weeks at the end of the dry season.

Redistribution, the direction of public affairs, internal security, and the defence of the group against external threats, are the governmental functions that are adduced to justify the material privileges of rulers. Can one weigh the respective contributions and conclude with Balandier that, all things considered, the price that holders of power should pay 'is never paid in full'[7]?

In many traditional African societies, the rulers' balance sheet does indeed show a deficit. They have not paid the price of their privileges. The accumulation of reserves for lean periods, the administration of justice and the maintenance of the public peace, require coercive power only in large, heterogeneous, urbanised societies. Elsewhere, the lineage network and its non-coercive sanctions are enough. The size of many traditional societies which have governments would not seem to have called for a monarch.

Chaka (*below*), king of the Zulus in the late nineteenth century, is a case, rather exceptional in Africa, of absolutist monarchy indistinguishable from despotism. In West Africa, the development of absolute monarchies into despotic rule seems to be an indirect consequence of the slave trade.

Right An eighteenth-century engraving of the evils of the slave trade.

There is still the problem of defence against external aggression. This aggression was a serious threat to black peasants during the period of the Atlantic slave-trade (from the sixteenth to nineteenth centuries), or when such conquerors as the Zulu king Chaka killed the people they conquered and took women and children as prisoners, or when human sacrifices of many victims were ritually organised in Benin and Dahomey. But at other times and places, from the fifteenth to the nineteenth centuries in the southern savanna kingdoms of the Luba, Lunda and Kuba, and in the states of the Nyoro, Ganda and Rundi in the Great Lakes area, foreign conquest meant no more to the villagers than a change in the beneficiaries of the taxes and dues imposed upon them.

With the exception of the redistribution we have spoken of, the rulers in traditional society drained away the surplus without giving anything of economic value in return. The non-economic services they rendered, such as the assurance of law and order, although indispensable in large urban societies, or when the group was being threatened by invaders, seem to have been superfluous in a good

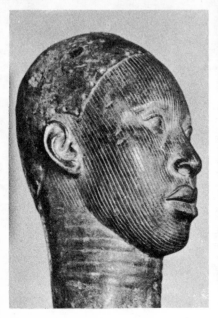 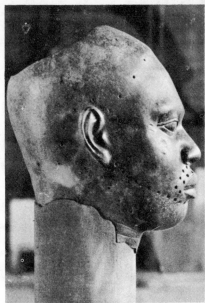

many African situations. One realises that the political network is a mediator of power relations. Rulers, by virtue of their control of the means of applying pressure, could establish relations of domination between themselves and their subjects.

The collective representations of politics

The African political enterprise, composed of coercion and interests, created very lofty and noble images of monarchy. The king or chief, from the very first moment of their accession to power, were supremely sacred, in the strongest sense of the word. Their life was closely bound up with the life of their people. If an ageing monarch became feeble, the army would be less powerful in combat, the women less fertile, men less virile, herds less numerous, and harvests less abundant. In some societies, the king had to poison himself, or allow himself to be poisoned, to prevent such a

Two thirteenth-century bronze heads
from Ife. Eighteen of these heads were
unearthed in 1938–9 near the palace of Oni,
king of Ife. (Ife Museum, Lagos).

community disaster. This sacrifice would be carried out in secret. As far as the people were concerned, the king did not die – he went to sleep, as it was said in kingdoms around the Gulf of Benin, or he was changed into various animals one after another, as was supposed in East African pastoral monarchies.

Interregna were periods of a type of crisis which was institutionalised (in the sense that provision was made for disorders that were expected and followed a predictable course) but which was nonetheless fraught with anxiety. Only when a new monarch had been installed could nature's and man's life resume its course again.

This sacred personage was not accountable to any human authority. His rights were absolute, because no others could be opposed to them. This absolutist theory was clearly expressed in the prosperous and highly centralised Sudanic kingdoms on the one hand, and the high plateaux of the east on the other: land, fields, men and animals all belonged to the king: he could at all times dispose of the life and property of his subjects without any justification. In practice, the exercise of his royal prerogatives was obviously limited by the balance of forces existing within the society at any given moment: the opposition of rival dynastic factions among the rulers, or passive resistance which could go as far as an exodus on the part of the subjects. But we are not interested here in these conditions, which are common to the working of all governments. We are only trying to describe the representations of political power made by traditional African societies.

Legitimacy was based on hereditary succession from a first king who founded the dynasty. He himself was usually considered a descendant of the gods, or one of their representatives on earth. Dynastic heredity was usually traced through males, whether the whole society followed the patrilineal principle, or only the dynasty adopted it. Such was the case in the kingdom of Kongo. Undoubtedly the kings there preferred to pass on the important royal office to their own sons rather than their sister's sons. The king's successor then was one of his sons, though not necessarily the eldest. This gave the king a certain measure of choice, and gave rise to much intrigue among his different wives' kinship groups. As legitimacy rested on a direct line of ascent to the founding king, *coups d'état* that ruptured this ideal genealogy were carefully camouflaged. In the interlacustrine kingdoms, the manipulation of history often took the following form: when the king's son is still a young child he is kidnapped, taken to another state, and brought up incognito; his personal bravery attracts the attention of the sovereign of this state, he offers the young man command of a group of warriors and gives him the hand of one of his daughters in marriage; the young man then returns to his native land at the head of his warriors, reveals his identity, gets rid of the usurper and becomes king in his turn. This charming tale in fact conceals a conquest, and confers legitimacy on the conqueror's descendants by reconnecting them to a lineage which had been deposed.

Do Africans conceive of their chiefdoms and kingdoms as states? In Western thought, this term refers to two concepts, one of a philosophical nature, and the other empirical. In the philosophical sense, particularly emphasised in the nineteenth century, the state is an ideal entity, the perfect form of society, it is endowed with a sort of will of its own. It is contrasted on the one hand with society, which is in some sense its more or less amorphous body, and, on the other hand, with the church, considered by Catholic thinkers to be another perfect social form. As Laurence Krader remarks, it is made into 'an object of reverence both for its intellectual appeal and for its brute coercive forces'. This kind of speculation is alien to African thought. According to it a common life-stream runs through all members of the same society, starting with the monarch who is the intelligence, will and life *par excellence* of the community.

In its empirical sense, notably in political science, the state is a complex institution of government endowed with sovereignty. The meaning used here belongs to that context; it is a permanent organisation of rulers. A society is not a state if it has only intermittent government; that is to say, where agents of force are recruited only to meet a crisis. Obviously, this is a question of the anthropologists' conceptual tools. As far as we are concerned, chiefdoms and kingdoms which maintain a permanent apparatus of constraint (in practice nearly all) are states, even if they are small in size. But this anthropological category, which is very applicable to Africa, has no part (as far as we know) in its collective representations.

The supreme ruler is characterised by his sacredness, absolute rights, and hereditary legitimacy. But even when coercive power was shared (albeit unequally) between rulers, these three characteristics of the monarch were not. As regards the third – hereditary legitimacy – those who had attained important political office certainly wished to pass it on to their heirs. On the other hand, the monarch sought to retain his right to appoint officials. The practice in fact generally oscillated between these two poles, depending on how successful the king was in implementing his will: when the balance of forces was in his favour, he chose successors; when he was unable to do this, he had to accept certain claims to inherit office. An intermediate solution was for the central authority to give his consent to an official's choice of successor.

Anthropological descriptions of the recruitment of rulers too often adopt an exclusively legalistic point of view. We are told, for example, that the king could choose anyone at all for political office. This is true in the sense that he was not obliged to choose a bureaucrat with specific qualifications. But this did not mean that all his subjects had an equal chance of being chosen. The men who had the greatest probability of being chosen were those the king knew personally, or those who were backed by important courtiers, or belonged to powerful lineages; while for an unknown, however

brilliant and talented, the probability was practically nil. Among non-rulers, the existence of a sort of reserve of potential recruits for political office was a crucial factor for both social advancement and the stability of the régime.

Rulers and subjects in colonial Africa

The colonial conquest of the nineteenth century was overtly political. It aimed at substituting one group of rulers for another in the political systems. It led, moreover, at first without explicitly intending it, to the replacement of traditional political systems by other much wider ones. This happened because, as we mentioned in the beginning, traditional global societies were slowly giving way

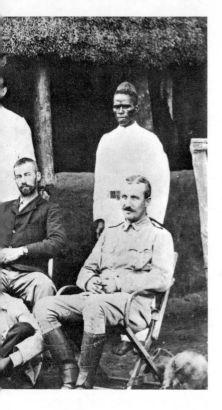

From the beginning of the colonial period, a convergence of interests united the large European commercial companies, the colonial administrations and the former local political authorities. In this picture, taken in Barotseland in the early years of the century, are assembled the executives of the British South Africa Company, Sir R. T. Coryndon, Administrator of North Western Rhodesia from 1900 to 1907, and Chief Lewanika.

to new global societies, each one covering a colonial territory. These changes in no way invalidate our model of elementary political relations. It applies just as well to colonial Africa as to traditional Africa.

The supreme ruler of the colony, usually holding the title of Governor General, was delegated by rulers from another global society, the metropolis (we do not consider metropolis and colonies as forming a single global society; this combination does not meet any of the criteria of the global society, see page 14). The most important actors in the metropolitan government (king or president, parliament and executive) were foreigners, and only exercised political power over the colony at the highest level (constitutional, legislative and international), giving a very large part of the executive, regulatory and even judiciary power to the Governor General. He, in turn, had his decisions carried out by a hierarchical body of rulers, or delegated his prerogatives to them. They made up a pyramid of bureaucratic type in which each official was appointed by some higher authority to whom he was responsible.

All the rulers in the higher echelons of the hierarchy were foreigners, members of the metropolitan society. Africans were sometimes appointed at lower levels. Agents exercising force (policemen, soldiers) were Africans, and their officers expatriates.

In some colonies or colonial areas, traditional rulers were integrated into the colonial hierarchy. This was the case with the Emirates of Northern Nigeria and Rwanda-Urundi. In this régime of so-called indirect rule, the chiefs or traditional kings continued to govern their kingdoms and chiefdoms. Of course their activity was closely controlled, and they were now no more than subordinate rulers, at the same time both executing the decisions of the Governor General and acting as representatives of their former subjects. *Vis-à-vis* the ruling group, who controlled the means of constraint and were economically privileged, the subjects were very heterogeneous. The one criterion of subject status was residence in the colonial territory. The subjects differed in cultural affiliations and identification with traditional societies, in nationality (metropolitan or other), in racial classification. But in all the Black African colonies, practically the whole subject population (more than 95 per cent and often reaching 98 to 99 per cent) consisted of members of chiefdoms and kingdoms whose territories had been incorporated into the colony.

Governing and administering a colony

Decisions in public affairs, from the whole colony to the smallest local community, rested with the rulers. People have often spoken of colonial paternalism. If one understands by this an attitude on the part of the authorities which, like a father towards his young children, decides everything, even details and trifles, 'for the good' of the people, without taking their opinion into account, the colonial rulers were certainly this way inclined. This attitude arose from the 'civilised' peoples' naïve belief, often well-intentioned, in their own superiority over these 'big children', and sometimes from the pleasure of dominating which undoubtedly attracted certain types of personality toward colonial administration. Whatever it was, it was only in the post-1945 phase of the colonial régime when it was felt that the end was at hand, that subjects were authorised to express their opinions on questions which directly concerned them. Advisory councils were set up at all governmental levels, newspapers were started, and political parties timidly emerged.

Internal security and defence against external threat were very effectively organised by the rulers. Public order reigned. The few revolts attempted at the beginning of the colonial period could offer no resistance to the superior arms of the rulers and the energy of the repression. External threats, that is threats from other colonies, were rare. The first expeditions, in the last quarter of the nineteenth century, looked at each other with hostility and distrust (those of Stanley and Savorgnan de Brazza, for example, on both sides of the Congo) but they avoided direct confrontation. During the 1914–18 war, there were Allied campaigns against the German colonies of Black Africa, but these campaigns exhibited none of the fury and savagery of the battles on the European front.

Besides these three functions of decision-making, peace, and defence, which, as we have seen, were also fulfilled by the traditional rulers, the colonial rulers gave considerable thought to what might be called the management of the society. The economic infrastructure (road and railway systems, ports and airports), the school system, hospitals and medical services, agricultural and veterinary

Chapel of Prophet Harris at Bregbo, Ivory Coast. Prophet Harris, a preacher at the beginning of the twentieth century, organised a cult which combined elements of Christianity with traditional rituals. It was looked on with suspicion by the colonial authorities who considered it a form of concealed resistance to their rule.

institutions were the activities which they directly managed. Every modern state has extended its activities into fields that were previously untouched (e.g. social security or unemployment insurance) or that were the responsibility of other institutions (e.g. hospitals run by religious orders). But this extension of governmental functions seems to have been taken further in the colonies than in the metropolitan countries. There was also a closer integration of these administrative services into the political network than in Europe. Physicians, veterinary surgeons, agronomists and teachers were officials, sometimes obliged to wear uniform and entitled to invoke the sanction of force more or less directly.

And, as everywhere else, the rulers imposed taxes and dues. Poll-taxes (that is, each man paying annually an identical sum) were easily imposed in the colonies. But as monetary incomes increased, this form of taxation was replaced by a proportional or progressive tax. At the beginning of colonisation, when currency was still not very widespread, statutory labour was exacted from colonial subjects. This manpower was used for public works (railway and road maintenance) but it was also sometimes put at the disposal of private plantations. Later on, in periods of crisis, colonial rulers again employed compulsory labour; for example, in the production drive during the Second World War.

Obedience of the subjects to the rulers' orders, which is the political relation in the raw, was secured by a very visible apparatus of constraint. While in the traditional political networks – as well as those of the metropolitan country at the time of colonisation – force was resorted to indirectly and as a last resort, in the colonies it was always present. Nobody troubled about persuasion; the punishment for disobedience was simply indicated.

Subjects did have some ways of resistance open to them, but revolts such as those of Matabele of Rhodesia in 1893 and 1896 quickly showed the futility of that kind of resistance. Consequently,

during most of the colonial period, African resistance was passive
and transposed. A reaction which was not concerted, but, because
it was spontaneous, was general, this passive resistance accounts,
in our view, for the well-known 'idleness of the natives' that
the colonial rulers complained of. One could hardly expect
heavy forced labour, of no obvious immediate utility, to be done
with zeal and enthusiasm. Transposed resistance is that which took
the form of religious movements (such as the Harris movement of
the western coastal regions and the Kibangism of Central Africa),
which looked to the arrival of a Messiah who would completely
reverse the order of things and suddenly establish a Golden Age.
These millenarian movements were usually authentically religious
in character; they were not covers for organisations of political

Joseph Munongo, chief of the Yeke, presiding at court
surrounded by the elders in his capital village
of Bunkeya. The architectural style of the building
typifies the colonial conception of village
buildings intended for use by Africans.

contest. But they expressed a refusal to accept the existing state of affairs in the society, which obviously included the colonial régime, and were in this sense objectively subversive. The colonial governments were under no illusions about these movements. Dissident churches and messianic cults were closely watched or even forbidden. After the Second World War, subjects could show resistance more openly, by strikes for example. Even so, it was not until independence was imminent that opposition to colonial governments as such could be expressed.

The ideology of political colonisation

The collective representations of the colonial enterprise varied. Each of the groups concerned (the African subjects, the colonial rulers, the European leading groups, metropolitan public opinion) saw the establishment of a political empire in Africa from its own point of view.

To the Africans, who were henceforth subject to foreign rule, it appeared first and foremost as a conquest. Superiority of arms, technical know-how and wealth had assured victory for the conquerors. They had then settled down to reap the benefits of their conquest. To the Africans this was painful but understandable. But as the period of military expeditions become more remote, subject status lost its legitimacy and seemed less and less bearable.

Colonial governments saw justification for their situation in the work they were accomplishing. They had brought peace to regions which had formerly been perpetually troubled by 'bloody tribal wars'. They administered even-handed justice to people who previously expected only corruption and torture; they organised efficient administrative machinery where there had been nothing but disorder. For the governing circles in the colonising countries, access to natural resources was essential for national expansion,

and this could only be achieved, at that particular moment of history, by political domination. What 'sacred egoism' required was clearly legitimate.

Finally, for particularly idealistic sections of public opinion in the metropolitan country, the colonial governments were accomplishing a 'civilising mission'. Their action made possible teaching, evangelisation and the spread of morality among peoples hitherto ignorant, superstitious and barbaric.

These different collective representations of colonial political power were sincerely held by most (perhaps all) Europeans. They were no less ideological for that. These justifications concealed two essential functions of the colonial political system: to maintain the economic integration of the metropolis and its African possessions, and to maintain a 'sphere of influence' *vis-à-vis* other industrial nations.

Even if, from the societal point of view, metropolis and colony formed two distinct societies, from the economic point of view

Political divisions 1970

they were a single system. The two parts of this system had different but complementary roles. The colony provided cheap raw materials (unskilled labour was plentiful and wages low), the metropolis transformed these materials into finished products, and the colony imported different goods from the mother country (from rails and railway equipment to soap and cotton goods). This familiar schema of the economic integration of colony and metropolis is naturally much simplified. One should add to it particularly the employment of European personnel for middle range and higher technical and administrative functions, and the high returns on capital invested by the metropolitan country. The privileged economic position enjoyed by citizens of the colonial power for seventy-five years was only made possible in Black Africa by political domination.

The nature of the second essential function of this domination of overseas territories was geopolitical. In Western diplomatic confrontation a nation's 'weight' depended on its 'empire'; that is to say, the totality of territories subject to its rule, which formed the main constituent of its sphere of influence.

Presidents and citizens in independent states

As we said in the first chapter, it was colonies that became independent, and not traditional political units. This peculiarity, albeit inevitable, has made the heads of states the heirs of the colonial governor generals. The definition of the role of independent rulers is strongly influenced both by the recent colonial past and by the traditional collective representations, which themselves belong to a time not so very distant.

The supreme ruler is the president. Two or three modern Black African kingdoms (such as Burundi and Buganda) were not able to maintain their constitutional kings. The role of the first heads of state of the young republics was legally defined in the constitutions of their

In the new independent States, presidents
and citizens replace rulers and subjects.
Left Jomo Kenyatta, President of Kenya, and
below Julius K. Nyere, President of Tanzania.

various countries. These different constitutions, drawn up by European jurists at the very end of the colonial period, established parliamentary régimes with separation of powers. An assembly, elected by universal suffrage, formed the legislature; a council of ministers, appointed by the president but responsible to parliament, directed administration; a judicial hierarchy, with the supreme court at the head, administered justice. The president, as the final arbiter, represented national sovereignty, but only enjoyed a very limited right of decision. The election of members of the assembly was to take place at regular, prescribed intervals; and a plurality of parties was considered necessary for the normal functioning of the system.

But in fact the African presidents did not play this relatively modest role for long. The first presidents, heroes of anti-colonial struggle, had enough personal prestige for their views to prevail. But very soon the constitutional institutions were working badly, and various vicissitudes produced the same result almost everywhere: a one-party presidential régime. The president assumes the functions of both head of state and prime minister, parliamentary control becomes a mere formality or is even suppressed. When the assembly is dissolved, special peoples' or military tribunals judge political offences. All political parties but one are forbidden.

This evolution, which may be said to be common to the Black African states, only took a few years, generally less than five. It is certainly derived from the collective representations of the traditional monarchy; for the peasant masses the man at the head of the political system has the right to be obeyed. Counterbalancing authorities are suspected of insubordination, and a critical opposition party is seen as subversive. It is derived also from the experience of the colonial political hierarchy; there too the political system was monolithic, simply questioning an order amounted to sedition, and public expression of a dissenting opinion was deemed an act of rebellion.

Below the president, ministers, heads of specialised departments, government representatives in provinces and districts, form the higher echelon of rulers; each in his own field enjoying wide powers of decision. Numerous subordinate agents are responsible for the execution of the measures adopted. Under colonial rule the body of civil servants constituted the sole group of rulers, because they alone could exercise the sanction of constraint. In independent Africa, the civil servant continues to be the backbone of the political relations system, but he is no longer alone. Military and party cadres also have to be classed among the rulers.

In the West, the term 'party' suggests competition for governmental roles. In Africa, the single party, by definition, allots these roles. It aims at creating political awareness in young people and those sections of the population (women and villagers) who previously lacked it. It tries, too, to exert constant pressure on the administration, so that they follow the party line in public affairs. A party could realise the above objectives by propaganda and by the sanctions of collective opinion. The party, in fact, can generally impose coercive sanctions both directly (through its militia or 'political police') and indirectly (through top party officials who also occupy high positions in the civil service). In contrast to Eastern European countries, where an elaborate practice and doctrine of relations between the communist party and the administration has been worked out, the situation in the African republics remains confused. Since there is no model to refer to, the single party often seems to be just one faction within the group of rulers.

From our point of view, the army is always included in the group of rulers. For even if its avowed function is the defence of the society from outside enemies, it is always internally an instrument of force. In both the traditional and colonial periods, the army was almost always part of a well-integrated group of rulers. It took its orders from the superior rulers and executed these orders by the

Learning the new procedures involved
in an election (for the sub-chiefs'
councils in Rwanda, 1956).

use of force. In the independent states today, the army constitutes
a separate body among the rulers, and is very aware of its own
identity. It reckons to judge the way the other rulers are performing
their roles, and eventually, if 'the national interest calls for it',
replaces them. In six years, from 1963 to 1968, there were seventeen
military *coups d'état* in independent Black Africa.

The present rulers in each global society thus form a heterogeneous
group, of which the three parts – civil service, party and army – are
also politically competitive factions even while they co-operate.

At the other end of the scale of political relations, the subjects
obey and pay their taxes. As citizens, collectively they are at the
source of all power, and as individuals they exercise by means of
elections the right to choose members of parliament and presidents.
But in fact, the suspension of assemblies, the disregard of constitutions, the assumption of special powers, the declaration of emerg-
encies, have reduced the control of government by the people to an
illusion. Citizens are, in fact, subject to a control which is visible
and permanent in the towns, though much more flexible and intermittent in the villages.

There are effective means of protection against this constraint.
An individual may exploit factional rivalries by becoming a
dependent of some important member of one faction. This,
obviously, is not without its dangers. For larger numbers of
subjects who feel themselves victims of coercive measures, resistance to the government has taken the form of armed revolt (like
that of Pierre Mulele of Congo-Kinshasa, or that in the Equatorial
Province of Sudan) or of secession (as in Biafra).

In addition to the usual tasks of government (decision-making, the
keeping of order, etc.), the rulers of African states undertake two
others: the direction of economic development, and the expression
of various trends within the global society. The problem of
economic development is of direct concern to rulers in Black

Africa. They make the basic decisions, set up programmes, and issue decrees (the administrative hierarchy); they explain the aims of austerity measures, and try to create some enthusiasm for the project (the party); they participate in collective tasks, and organise the population which does the work (the army). Furthermore, as there are still few specialised organisations such as professional associations expressing particular orientations of thought and action, the government acts as spokesman, especially overseas, for its physicians, artists, etc.

Bases of legitimacy

There are different ways of attaining governmental roles. At the summit, the alternatives are constitutional procedure or *coup d'état*. The presidents elected immediately after independence were usually appointed according to the rules set down in the charter. Their legitimacy was based on legality, but also, and perhaps even more so in the eyes of the people, on their leadership during the struggle at the end of the colonial régime. Presidents Nkrumah (Ghana), Kenyatta (Kenya), Sékou Touré (Guinea), Modibo Keita (Mali), Senghor (Senegal), Houphouët-Boigny (Ivory Coast), Kasavubu (Congo-Kinshasa), having been the figureheads of the liberation movements, had some sort of a right to continue their mission once independence was achieved.

The men, generally soldiers, who attained the presidency by *coup d'état* sometimes tried to change the constitution so as to legalise their own position. But they all assert that their basic legitimacy is derived from the sheer necessity of taking action to safeguard national interests endangered by the corrupt or ill-directed management of the previous government. The rhetoric of the presidents who have seized power by force invokes either the restoration of order in a situation of political and economic anarchy, or the revolution to establish a new social order which will be just, fraternal and socialist. This is no more than rhetoric, for there are few African régimes that do not claim to be socialist (whatever, in fact, are their basic political and economic choices) and few *coups d'etat* that do not pretend to be revolutionary (even when it is only a question of the victory, often ephemeral, of a ruling faction seeking to occupy the summit of the hierarchy).

But there are other positions than the very highest in the political hierarchy. How does one acquire medium and lower governmental positions? In strictly graded organisations such as the civil service and army, people usually enter by competitive examination, and progress from one grade to the next either by passing the tests marking each stage, or by seniority, or by showing exceptional ability which is rewarded by faster promotion. It is somewhat easier to get into the party, where zeal and loyalty assure one's advancement.

These then are the rules. But the political network is not isolated from other networks: kinship and marriage play a part in winning important positions and promotion within the ruling group; lineage solidarity creates obligations which people do not like to evade; a ruler in a high position has to help a member of his family advance his career. Only very 'progressive' Africans and foreigners to the continent find this shocking. The others 'understand'. The high ranking official who favours his brothers does not, then, incur a great degree of collective reprobation. By doing this he moreover acquires a clientage which is indispensible for the advancement of his own career: a group of devoted retainers, tied to a ruler by a relationship of personal dependence, makes it easier for him to get ahead. These clients are not all kin, to be sure. But many are, and the ties of choice and blood reinforce one another. It is the same with affines. A sort of secondary, but very real kinship, affinity marks out individuals for the favour of the authorities and at the same time provides them with a guarantee of loyalty.

In modern Africa, painfully struggling to emerge from under-development and not everywhere succeeding, there are not many opportunities for young people who have completed secondary or university studies. The large foreign industrial and commercial concerns which could use their skills do not have enough employment to offer. Less important private enterprises (plantations, mechanical repair works, carpentry, small businesses) do not offer many openings either. There remains the civil service. Since it is so sought after, one cannot enter it or advance in it without the kind of support just mentioned.

6 Repetitive and dynamic models

In less than a century, Black Africa has known three cultural systems with total breaks between them. These changes were first apparent in political relations. It is true that colonisation and decolonisation can be explained in economic terms. But this is a matter of analysis. From the descriptive point of view, the colonial conquest first puts an end to traditional sovereignties, and the liberation of the colonies in turn ends the sovereignty of the metropolis and establishes the new sovereignties of independent states. On each occasion the role of the supreme ruler is redefined and thus a new political network is created. In the preceding chapter we described in turn the traditional, colonial and independent models of the political network. This succession of models corresponded to three phases of an historical development. But did it account for this historical development?

Our scheme seems to be open to the same kind of criticism that Balandier makes of structuralist research. According to him, political phenomena 'because of their synthesising or all-encompassing nature, and of their dynamic qualities . . . cannot be reduced to the kind of formal structures which the social sciences have used until now'. The structuralist schema which 'fixes what is essentially dynamic . . . cannot be satisfactorily applied to complex and unstable systems of relations'[1].

The model as field of force

Every description of dynamic processes which uses the written word, diagrams or drawings, is translating something moving into something which is necessarily static. An historian who seeks to recreate the concrete development of a succession of events describes its most significant moments. His account is like a series of snapshots. In order to get closer to the evolution of the facts he is relating, he can multiply these moments as a draftsman might multiply drawings of dance-steps to get a sequence. But whatever happens, the outcome is inevitably something fixed and static. The anthropologist in his analysis proceeds along similar lines. His account will be at a more abstract level, for, unlike the historian, he is not studying a single sequence, but the results of comparing several cases. Models are the most meaningful configuration of characteristics common to several cases. Writing makes them static.

Balandier's criticism obviously does not apply to the kind of stability inherent in the very way one makes a model. In our view it has more bearing on the inertia of the model: the fact that, left to itself, a model stays indefinitely in the same state. A king commands and subjects obey, the king's successor commands and the subjects' descendants obey, and so on. The model only seems to account for this interminable repetition. But as we know from other sources that this repetition will one day be interrupted, and its model replaced by another model, we might as well admit with Balandier that this change remains unexplained.

But not all models are inert and repetitive. Some represent fields in which various forces are in constant opposition. Insofar as they neutralise each other, the model remains basically stable. Evolution occurs when one force is somewhat stronger than another. When the imbalance is too great, there is a break and the model disappears. Our models are of this dynamic type.

In the traditional political model, rulers and subjects were in constant opposition, and sometimes the rulers themselves split into two factions. There are the forces of change (the rulers always want to extract more from their subjects, who want to give as little as possible; the faction containing the most rulers wants to maintain and increase its advantages, and the minority faction wants to become the majority). Often the two lines of tension do not remain separate, but combine into a single opposition: either the minority faction and subjects join forces against the majority faction, or, in the face of pressure from the subjects, the two factions join forces to resist it. In small chiefdoms and kingdoms, the equilibrium point of the forces of coercion and resistance was fairly low: pressure from all sides was weak. Rulers could not lay their hands on very much (in view of the level of production and the number of subjects); subjects did not have to put much energy into resistance (they were protected by the kinship network, and the necessarily direct relationship they maintained with rulers). As political units grow bigger, the stakes become more important and the coercion stronger; the balance which is reached is less favourable to the subjects than it was in chiefdoms and small kingdoms. It would be even less so if the dynasty was not forced to devote some of its resources to self-defence against the political ambitions of important lineages.

Thus there was some evolution within the traditional political model because of the constant fluctuations of the opposing forces. It nonetheless continued without breaking. It undoubtedly owes its solidity to the absence of important changes in traditional African cultures. A new production technique or written language could have changed the political model, so long as the rulers did not appropriate them to strengthen their own position. This, in fact, was characteristic of the pre-colonial contacts with the outside world: the rulers of the city states of the Sudanese savanna reaped all the benefits of trans-Saharan trade with the Maghreb; the chiefs of the states of the west coast were the ones who profited from the slave trade with the New World; the Central African rulers monopolised the guns which the Arab traders exchanged for copper and ivory.

Be that as it may, it was an external event – the colonial conquest – which put an end to the traditional political network. There was tension from the start in the colonial model itself, between the two opposing forces. Considerable coercion had to be used to put an end to attempted revolts and, above all, passive resistance. But for a time, equilibrium was established. Then the subjects' resistance grew stronger. Unequal access to goods, segregation measures and the absence of any participation in public affairs, at first accepted without too much trouble, became less and less bearable as new collective representations gained ground. These were engendered by the colonial society itself. On the one hand, the monetary economy, the abundance of imported consumer goods, and the Europeans' high and very visible standard of living, gave people a taste for the good things money could buy, but which were inaccessible to workers at low wages. On the other hand, education gave people access to the major trends of thought of the industrial age, young people participated in these developments, and discovered the appeal of such hackneyed words as liberty, equality and socialism. To maintain the colonial political network, the rulers had to balance the forces of resistance by increasing coercion. This was the course taken by the Portuguese rulers. Elsewhere, for various reasons, metropolitan governments did not want to keep the balance of forces at a very high level of tension. The colonial political model broke down from its own internal dynamism.

As we have seen, the independent political model is an unstable one. Various forces meet there, and the resulting equilibrium is precarious. The simple opposition of rulers and ruled is not enough to account for this. Different groups, each with their own interests, are in conflict; besides the decision-makers, administrative officials, party cadres and military already mentioned, there are the descendants of pre-colonial authorities, the chiefs who were integrated in the colonial hierarchy the lower-ranking officials of the colonial régime, the trade unions, the small businessmen, etc.

Furthermore, group interests are not the only forces active within the field of the model. There are other kinds of force, different but equally active. These are the cultural constants which

are undoubtedly deeply rooted in the human psyche. Cultural continuity, the tendency for forms to persist even when their original context has disappeared, also enters in the political domain. This continuity maintains lineage solidarity among the rulers, it creates political parties based on tribal loyalties, it ensures the survival of colonial paternalism in political relations, of the authoritarianism of kings and rulers and their distrust of all opposition. Another constant is coherence: the tendency for the culture of a total society to form, at any given moment, a relatively integrated whole (whatever may be the principles of this integration). Coherence is a force for change, for in order constantly to re-establish this sort of synchronic unity, it discards what it cannot assimilate (constitutional presidency without power of decision, for example) and rapidly adopts what is compatible (a one-party system, for example).

Our three political models do not have the stability of inertia. Being the result of a balance of forces in continual interaction, each model changes all the time, and sometimes breaks down. Like the historian or the draftsman, in order to show their inherent stability we have chosen times when the balance has been maintained for quite a long time, in spite of minor variations. But we know that this is only a snapshot in a moving process.

Permanent features of Africa political networks

Even if historical models of concrete networks vary, the elementary political relation, which is also a model, has proved a solid and useful tool in the African field. It has enabled us to locate, define and analyse certain types of societal relations which are everywhere organised in a distinct network. Can one observe any permanent features in African networks? If the answer is yes, we may be tempted to extend the field of comparison and ask if these permanent features are characteristic of political networks.

Our point of departure having been a purely formal definition of political relations (those existing between rulers and ruled, and sanctioned by coercion), we had put off an examination of the functions of those relations until we had studied several networks – which we have now done.

The functions of the political network are not to be confused with the tasks of the rulers. The latter are observable and explicitly enumerated in the role which is culturally assigned to every ruler in a given society. The king decides the date of the first sowing; the head of a province judges cases; the district head collects taxes, etc. We have already described these tasks in a rather more abstract way (decisions in matters concerning the whole society, maintenance of internal peace, direction of economic development programmes, etc.). But these kinds of activity have a specific aim and are familiar to all members of the society. The functions which belong to the whole network are not directly observable but inferred, are not expressed in what Malinowski called the 'charter' of an institution and therefore remain largely unknown to the members of the society. What does the political network do in the societal system of which it is a part? What are its uses in the global society? When we have answered these questions, we shall have explained the functions of the political network.

We thus use function here in a wider sense than in the functional theories of Radcliffe-Brown (for whom function is a contribution to the maintenance of the society) and Malinowski (for whom the function of an element is its relation to other elements in the same culture; this, at least, is one of the senses Malinowski gave to function)[2].

The network, through which orders and assents to them circulate, operates to preserve the societal order as it exists at a given moment. Preserving the societal order is not the same thing as keeping a society alive; it means assuring the continuity of the *status quo* in all the sectors of social organisation: kinship and marriage; stratification and dependence; associations and economics. The societal order embodies, for instance, a specific system of distribution of goods, a specific institution of clientship. Changing these does not endanger the global society itself; on the contrary, often even a radical change in a network favours the development of the global society. To the societal order, systems of collective representations are linked: religious ideas, world views, ethics, bodies of knowledge, artistic styles, etc. The political network, in maintaining the societal order, also maintains the *status quo* in the collective representations. As beliefs, ideas and even styles are created or adopted by different groups within the societal order, new collective representations generally meet with opposition from the political network. The same thing applies to production techniques used by the economic network. They are maintained in their existing state.

We are not saying that rulers expressly set out to uphold the social and cultural *status quo*, nor that people who want to bring about changes cannot sometimes succeed; all we are saying is that what we have been able to learn about the African political network indicates that in itself it has a conservatory function.

This first function grows out of another, that of securing a privileged position for a minority of members of the global society. In traditional, colonial and independent Africa alike, rulers benefit more from consumer goods and services than the ordinary people they rule, and this without themselves taking part in any process of economic production and exchange. This remarkable result is obtained through the almost automatic functioning of the network. The subjects bring in the goods; these largely provide subsistence of the rulers; they are thus in a position to exercise constraint, and this is what enables them to obtain goods. And so the cycle goes on. This network is not isolated but is one among many. Together they form the changing but well-ordered fabric of societal relations. For any one of them to function efficiently, all must come into play. That is why the political system operates to maintain the societal order: the maintenance of the *status quo* is the best guarantee that the cycle of privileges will persist.

As we pass from the traditional to the colonial model, and from there to the independent model, we see that there is an increase in governmental tasks. Some of these are services which can be obtained for money and thus are economically assessable. This applies, for example, to the construction and maintenance of roads, medical and hospital services, and the development of natural

Colonial governments entered new areas of acitivity not
directly linked to the enforcement of law and order.
Here Bukavu school children are joining a State savings
institution organised by the Belgian colonial administration.

resources. The people in charge of these activities belong to the political network in the sense that they are paid by the Treasury out of public funds provided by taxes, and are able to call upon coercion if necessary. On the other hand, their wages and salaries are prestations which have an economic value since there is a market for this kind of service. This is an extension of the concept of political relations of which the distinctive features are easier to grasp in traditional Africa.

Indeed, when a government emerges in a small-scale society with a limited economic surplus, a direct relationship between constraint, concentration of the surplus and absence of economic returns is perceptible. These three elements are also present in more complex models, but their relationships are less direct and less obvious. They are hidden among other elements, and rulers do nothing to bring them to light.

From the African material we can draw two conclusions. First, the political network fulfils the function of preserving the existing societal order. Secondly, it secures goods for the rulers without any economic counterpart.

This second function of the political network corresponds to the definition of the power relation offered earlier. This explains why the power relation and the political relation are so often confused. Constraint is the most obvious and direct way of applying pressure; and it is, at the same time, the characteristic sanction of rulers. The acquisition of goods and services without corresponding return is institutionalised in taxes and levies. The ruler is always dominant, the subject always dominated, and the relation of government is always one of power. But one cannot reverse these propositions. The dominant is not always a ruler, the dominated not always a subject, and the relation of power not always a relation of government. That is why we distinguished very clearly between power and politics.

Having made that distinction, we must emphasise that the political network acts as the ideal support for relations of power. Other relations – kinship, marriage, inequality or dependence – can also be used as mediators of power, but in a less direct and complete way than the relation of government. Consequently, men who wish to dominate try to climb to the summit of the government hierarchy. A scheme of power relations which limits the satisfactions of the dominant to purely material benefits can be justified only by methodological necessity. Power has certainly other attractions than those of material goods. Our method, unfortunately, does not allow us to investigate these.

7 Inequality

Kinship, marriage and government constitute networks which, in our experience, are unavoidable. If we could imagine a society with free and unrestricted social relations, we should have to admit that this was Utopian. It is a different matter with social inequality. Even if we ordinarily experience it, then it is, at least for twentieth-century Western man, an anomaly and an injustice. As Louis Dumont so well argued, there should be no *homo hierarchicus* for us, but only the *homo aequalis*[1]. What can we learn from Africa about the equality of members of the same society?

In the broadest sense, units are equal when they are of the same quantity, quality, intensity or value; in a nutshell, when they exhibit one or more identical characteristics. Equality is based on the identity of features of the units one is comparing. There can be a great number of identical features, as in objects made by mass-production, for example. But naturally there will always be some differences, if only that two cars coming off the same conveyor belt cannot be at the same place at the same time.

Inequality, in this sense, has little significance in relation to members of a society. Concrete characteristics, physical or mental, taken separately, are rarely identical in any two individuals, and taken together they never are. Consequently, one has to use another frame of reference in approaching the phenomena of social inequality. One must not start from identical or different characteristics, but from the relations (of groups, not individuals) which divide a single society. It is from this point of view that philosophers and historians, sociologists and anthropologists, have tackled social inequality. From Plato to St Thomas Aquinas, from Rousseau to Marx, from Max Weber to Talcott Parsons, it has always been a question of the relationship between aristocrats, citizens and slaves; between nobles, commoners and peasants; between priests, warriors, merchants and servants; between capitalists and proletarians.

The elementary model of inequality/equality

In Western Europe in the Middle Ages, when two strangers engaged in conversation the most important thing for each was to know the status of the other. Was he a nobleman or a commoner, a cleric or a serf? Each man would behave as a superior, an equal or an inferior towards the person he was speaking to, according to the culturally defined rank of their respective statuses.

In order for there to be societal inequality between two actors, their society as a whole must be divided into hierarchical groups, and each of the actors must belong to a different group. In any graphic representation of such a society, these groups would correspond to horizontal divisions recalling the geological strata in the cross-section of a terrain. This indeed is the reason why one generally calls these horizontal divisions of a society 'strata'. Social strata are hierarchical and ranked, just as geological strata are superimposed. A *rank* is the relative position of a unit in a series of units of the same type. For a society to be stratified, there must be at least two ranked strata.

The *status* of one actor in relationship to another (superior, inferior, equal) is determined solely by the stratum he belongs to. In a society divided into three strata, A, B and C, all those who belong to stratum B have the same status, and consequently are socially equal to one another, while they are inferior to members of stratum A and superior to those of stratum C. Just as belonging to a global society at the present time confers the same nationality on an individual without any gradation (one either has British nationality or one doesn't have it; Brown does not have it more than Smith and a little less than Jones), belonging to a stratum confers the same status on all the individuals. Individual differences of physical or mental qualities, innate or acquired, of wealth, earned or inherited, of reputation or influence, have no bearing on status as we understand it. The word status has several other meanings, equally legitimate with the one advanced here; but for analytical purposes, its use here is restricted to the very special sense we have just defined.

The elementary relation of social stratification is defined in terms of the actors' status. The relation of equality unites actors of the same status, while relations of superiority and inferiority unite actors of different status. Every stratified society has as part of its cultural heritage an enumeration of the ways in which equals, superiors and inferiors are expected to behave. They are the roles to which people are obliged to conform. Those who refuse to conform always risk collective reprobation and sometimes even legal sanctions. Thus during certain periods of the Roman Empire, the European Middle Ages and the Tokugawa shogunate of Japan, the quality, colour and form of clothing of each social stratum were determined by law. Infraction of these rules was punished by the courts.

We are starting, as we did in our study of the other networks, with the formal relation which is very skeletal. Thus the basis of the hierarchy of strata remains indeterminate. This basis can be a specialised occupation (animal husbandry, agriculture, hunting; priesthood, war, commerce), or possession of goods (rich and poor), or relationship to the means of production (capitalist and proletarian) or descent (noble and commoner). The existence of a hierarchy among various groups is sufficient sign of an unequal society. Also indeterminate are ways of acquiring status (birth, marriage and personal activity), collective representations which explain inequality, and the functions of stratification in a society.

The model of inequality seems to be fundamental, since it cannot be reduced to the other elementary relations which are the basis of social networks. The model it is most often confused with is the political one. Relations of government and relations of inequality are both asymmetrical. One cannot reverse the roles of the two actors without changing the meaning of their relationship. In a symmetrical relationship – for example that of equality – since the actors' roles are identical, one can reverse them. Now most social relations are asymmetrical; father and son, brother and sister, husband and wife, etc. In these respects the political relation and the superiority/inferiority relation are very different: rulers can use coercion, whereas members of the superior strata cannot have recourse to it. The political network is almost universal in traditional Africa, as it is in the colonial and independent periods, whereas that of stratification is far less common. In societies where the two systems co-exist, they are very clearly distinguished: although all the rulers with power of decision belong to the superior stratum, not all the members of that stratum are rulers.

The concept of inequality here advanced allows one immediately to reply to a possible *a priori* objection. It is sometimes said that traditional societies could not but have been homogeneous, since differences of occupation, wealth and standards of living were slight. In the first place, this objection reveals a naïve ethnocentrism – these differences only seem unimportant and superficial to an outside observer. Furthermore, only two conditions are necessary for the foundation of a stratification system: first, that all members of the society could be classified into two categories according to any criterion whatsoever (not necessarily that of wealth); secondly, that one of these categories was considered to be superior to the other. Both these conditions can be met in any society.

The origin of inequality in the Great Lakes area

There were many stratified societies in traditional Africa. In the southern savanna states, there were both aristocrats and villagers among the Kongo, Kuba, Lunda and other kingdoms of the 'civilisations of the granaries'. In the corresponding region of the northern savanna where the 'civilisation of the cities' developed, most of the city-states were characterised by systems of social inequality. We know this through the Arab chroniclers who recorded the history of this area. It included Ghana, Mali, the seven Hausa cities, Bornu, etc. In societies of pastoral origin, of the 'civilisation of the spear', the kingdoms of the interlacustrine cultural area were noted for their particularly clear form of stratification. We have a better knowledge than we would normally have in Africa of the histories of these societies from the oral traditions which have been scrupulously preserved. We are thus able to grasp the genesis of their networks of inequality. We shall consider the stratification of four of these traditional societies in more detail: Ankole, Rwanda, Burundi and Buha.

The long geological rift which stretches from north to south from Juba on the Nile towards the mouth of the Zambesi clearly demarcates, in the latitudes close to the equator, the eastern boundary of the great rain forest of the Congo basin. In that gigantic fault were formed four large lakes: Albert, Edward, Kivu and Tanganyika. A mountainous chain rises on their eastern shores to a height of about 9,000 feet; this marks the line where the waters of the Congo and Nile divide. Leaving these summits, the contour of the land gets lower towards the East until finally we get to lakes Kyoga and Victoria (3,390 feet above sea level). Between these six lakes – the Great Lakes – there stretches a region of high plateaux with altitudes ranging from 3,000 to 4,500 feet. The vegetation is characteristic of grassland, with sparsely scattered trees except in the woods along the banks. The annual rainfall is 80–150 cm. The tsetse fly which transmit sleeping sickness to cattle are widespread only at lower altitudes. This combination of physical conditions makes the interlacustrine region a very favourable one for human habitation: one can practise agriculture and animal husbandry there, and easily move about from place to place. It offers a welcome to migrant peoples, who have easy access to it from the north.

The first inhabitants of the high plateaux were no doubt hunters of the negrillo type. They lived, like the neighbouring people of the equatorial forest who are still living there, by hunting and gathering. The second group entered from the north; they were Ethiopid herdsmen who migrated in several waves. The oldest of these belong to a very distant past, probably the beginning of the first millennium BC; the more recent probably go back no further than the twelfth and thirteen centuries AD. We know some of the names of these later invaders: Chwezi, Hima and Tutsi. From the beginning of the first centuries of the Christian era, a much more copious flow was added to the slow and sparse Ethiopid migrations, that of the Bantu-speaking cultivators who probably came from the north-west. Culturally and genetically absorbing the Ethiopid herdsmen – at least those who had arrived before them – the Bantu formed small agrarian chiefdoms on the most fertile lands – that is, on the banks of the lakes, in the valleys and at high altitudes with high precipitation. The last waves of Ethiopid nomad warriors established their kraals between these small peasant communities. During this process of settlement some lineages imposed their authority upon others, and became the dynasties of the chiefs and kings. Thus the Chwezi in the northern part of the interlacustrine area (in what is now Uganda) established the kingdom of Kitara, which dominated the region from approximately the thirteenth to fifteenth centuries. Thus the Tutsi also established several kingdoms in the south: Bugesera, Buganza, Gisaka and Rwanda. A fourth stream of migration after the negrillos, Ethiopids and Bantu, again entered the interlacustrine country from the north. Towards the end of the fifteenth century the Luo, Nilotic warrior herdsmen, toppled the Chwezi dynasty which they replaced with that of the

Bito, and the kingdom of Kitara became the kingdom of Bunyoro.

After the arrival of the Luo, the streams of migration into the Great Lakes area dried up but internal development continued in a very interesting way. The situation, from the sixteenth to the nineteenth centuries, is very fluid: some political units come into being, and others disappear. Some kingdoms divide while others expand. However, one can perceive two movements in these changes: one involves the kingdoms of warrior herdsmen and the relations between them; the other the relations between kingdoms and the peasant communities who live in the interstices of the system by the last waves of invaders.

The first movement takes place in several stages. First there is a sort of swarming from the centre, where a band of immigrants is settled. Thus Buganda was founded by a member of the dynastic lineage of Bunyoro. Then, after a certain time, they assert their independence by refusing to pay the usual tribute (this is what Buganda did to Bunyoro, and Rwanda to Bugesera). Then follows expansion by the annexation of other less aggressive or weaker kingdoms. At the end of the nineteenth century Rwanda was still pursuing its imperialistic policy[2].

The second movement, contemporary with the first, aimed at progressively securing complete control of the peasant population whose forebears had settled on the high plateaux before the arrival of the last Ethiopid or Nilotic herdsmen. The latter used several strategies but rarely, it seems, direct military conquest. The ascendancy which the invaders gained from their war-like reputation and the prestige of their wealth enabled them to arbitrate disputes between peasants, and to protect them from their own chiefs. They used other indirect and ingenious tactics too. The result of all this could be seen at the end of the traditional period; it continued right through the colonial period; and even independence did not everywhere destroy it: it was stratification.

A Luo elder. The Luo were the   145
last pastoralist invaders to
enter the Great Lakes area.

Four networks of stratification

At the end of the nineteenth century, the colonial conquest froze
the situation which until then had been fluid among the kingdoms
of the Great Lakes. From 1890 to 1910 explorers and soldiers,
travellers and missionaries were struck by the very obvious
heterogeneity of the subjects of the kings of Ankole, Rwanda,
Burundi, and the Buha chiefdoms.

This heterogeneity was shown in the groups into which the
populations of all these kingdoms were divided. These groups were
distinguished by their names. In Ankole there were the Hima and
the Iru; in Rwanda, the Tutsi, Hutu and Twa; in Burundi, the
Tutsi, Hima, Hutu and Twa; in Buha, the Tutsi and the Ha. Each
group traditionally had its appropriate occupation. The Hima and
Tutsi reared cattle, the Iru, Hutu and Ha cultivated the land, and
the Twa hunted, made pottery and were devoted servants of the
Tutsi. Distinctive physical characteristics were attributed to each
group; the Hima and Tutsi type was tall, slender-limbed and had a
thin nose. An Iru, Hutu or Ha was characterised by a stocky,
robust body build with thick-set features. The Twa were short with
broad shoulders. Clothes also emphasised the differences between
the groups. The Tutsi and Hima wore leather loin-cloths or light
coloured cotton tunics. The Hutu and Ha wore bark cloth, and the
Twa skins of wild animals. Each group differed from the others in
its domestic and social life, cults and ceremonies. Each was endogamous. In each society the two, three or four divisions were clearly
ranked in an order of superiority/inferiority. No individual
escaped this classification; everyone necessarily had to belong to
one of these hierarchical groups.

The elementary model of inequality undoubtedly applies to these
four networks. An examination of them very clearly demonstrates
the functioning of a traditional system of stratification. The brief

historical reconstruction previously outlined shows the importance of the hereditary principle. The three basic strata called by six names reflect the three different occupations of the three streams of immigrants. The Twa are the pygmoid descendants of pygmy hunters who were probably the first men to roam about the Great Lakes region. The Iru, Hutu and Ha are descendants of the peasant population composed to a large extent of Bantu invaders, and to a lesser degree of the first waves of Ethiopids. The Hima and Tutsi are descendants of the last Ethiopid bands who managed to maintain their identity instead of being absorbed by the agriculturalists. Only the fourth wave of immigrants, the Nilotic Luo herdsmen, is unrepresented in our networks of inequality. Ankole, Burundi and Buha are found south of the area conquered by the Luo. That is why we do not find there the Luo dynasty of Bito, but Ethiopid dynasties: the Nyiginya (in Rwanda), the Hinda related to the Chwezi (in Ankole and perhaps Burundi and Buha). The stratifications observed during the period 1890–1910 give us a picture, albeit incomplete, of an history which undoubtedly extends over more than two millennia.

Castes and classes

The fact that the descendants of these people to a large extent retained their ancestors' occupations, and even part of their genetic heritage, clearly shows that an individual does not become a member of a stratum during his lifetime; he is born into it. If one adds that each stratum is endogamous and separated from the others, one can conclude that we are, in fact, dealing with *caste* (the term is to be understood in the anthropological sense, with no reference to traditional India except that one can abstract the notion of a closed stratum from the Indian system, and then apply the term to all social phenomena which fit this description).

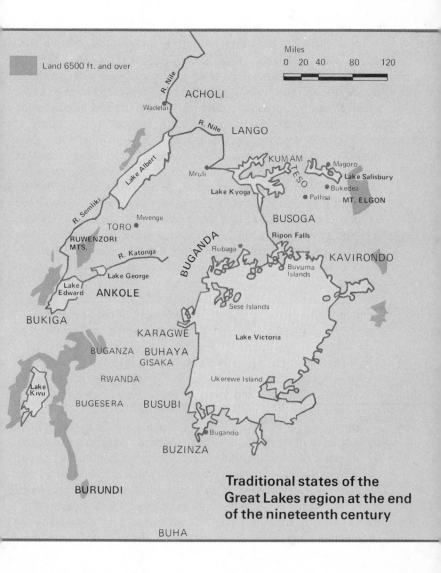

Miles

0 20 40   80   120

Land 6500 ft. and over

R. Nile

ACHOLI

Wadelai

R. Nile

LANGO

KUMAM

TESO

Magoro

Lake Salisbury

Lake Albert

Mruli

Lake Kyoga

Bukedea

Pallisa

MT. ELGON

R. Semliki

Mwenge

BUSOGA

TORO

Ripon Falls

RUWENZORI
MTS.

BUGANDA

KAVIRONDO

R. Katonga

Rubaga

Buvuma
Islands

Lake George

Lake
Edward

ANKOLE

Sese Islands

BUKIGA

KARAGWE

Lake Victoria

BUGANZA

BUHAYA

GISAKA

Lake
Kivu

RWANDA

Ukerewe Island

BUGESERA

BUSUBI

BUZINZA

Bugando

**Traditional states of the
Great Lakes region at the end
of the nineteenth century**

BURUNDI

BUHA

Twa singers in Rwanda. The Twa, who
constitute less than one per cent
of the Rwanda population, are the
lowest stratum of the society.

This conclusion is certainly valid for the pastoral stratum: one cannot gain admittance to it, it is closed; therefore it is a caste. But the highest stratum in a system can be closed without all the others being closed, or closed in the same way. One must examine each of them in turn. It is possible to enter the peasant stratum. A poor herdsman who has lost his cattle, is reduced to working on the land and marrying the daughter of a cultivator, becomes a peasant: one can fall from the first social class to the second. Can one climb from the third to the second? Even if a Twa cultivates land he remains a Twa because, in other peoples' eyes, the Twa are defined by 'race' rather than by hereditary occupation. Neither can anyone else become a Twa. A peasant who takes up hunting remains a peasant. It must be said that there are very few Twa; they only represent about one per cent of the population in Rwanda and Burundi; and there are none at all in Ankole and in the chiefdoms of Buha.

A word about the four-level system of Burundi: the Tutsi and Hima are both herdsmen, and probably both of the same Ethiopid origin. Nevertheless, they occupy different levels in the stratification. There is no intermarriage between them. The Tutsi (also known as Nyaruguru) practise endogamy, and can even marry into the princely families, those of a limited group of hereditary rulers, the Ganwa. The Tutsi and Hima of Burundi have sometimes been contrasted in terms of pure and impure caste.

Summing up, the four networks of inequality have in common their division into two major strata – the herdsmen and the peasants. The first is a caste, the second is a *class*. This last term is used here to describe a relatively open and less exclusive stratum; it does not refer to relations to production in an industrial society. One can ascribe numerous values to such concepts as openness or closedness, community and segregation. Thus caste and class are not opposed as two contradictory categories, but as the two poles of an axis with many

intermediary degrees. Like the herdsmen, the Twa stratum is a caste, but for other reasons.

Caste subcultures, personalities and myths

Each of the four societies had its own language spoken by the whole population. All the members of the same society also shared certain fundamental religious beliefs. With the exception of these two areas, each stratum had its own way of life, its own subculture: food and housing, body ornaments and decorative drawings, literature and music, ceremonies and dances. The superiority of the herdsmen caste is transmitted to its subculture. Because the Tutsi were characterised by mainly liquid diet (milk, banana beer and mead) the latter was considered more desirable than the solid

food of the peasants. Because the basketwork of the aristocratic women was decorated with austere, elongated shapes, simplicity of line was greatly appreciated and considered 'good taste'.

A hereditary caste favours certain attitudes, qualities and psychological traits. The warrior herdsmen, for example, set great store by self-control, personal courage, the sense of authority, group pride and haughty politeness. From their earliest years, children of superior status heard the possessors of these virtues praised and admired. As young men doing a military training of several years at the king's or a chief's court, their education was explicitly intended to develop these qualities. It is normal under these conditions for a 'caste personality' to emerge. This does not refer to basic personality structure, but to a configuration of

A traditional Tutsi war dance. The Tutsi infiltrated into the Great Lakes area from the thirteenth to the fifteenth centuries, and settled successfully in this area, thanks to their military superiority and possession of cattle.

characteristics which is commoner in one stratum than in another. There was no such educational mechanism in the peasant class. But other qualities made in practice for a better adaptation to the situation of an inferior: the external expression of respect and submission, prudence and perspicacity, endurance and dissimulation. As these traits, with their survival value in a stratified society, were 'rewarded' and so more or less consciously sought after, and as the aristocratic virtues were neither cultivated nor advantageous, there soon emerged a very different 'lower class personality'.

In these four interlacustrine societies, one can see that stratification was not a superficial phenomenon. The day to day reality of everyone's life, as well as the special occasions, was dominated by inequality of status. People have sometimes asked whether a society can be stratified 'without knowing it'. This question is usually asked about societies which explicitly condemn social inequality: Republican France, the United States, Soviet Russia. In a relationship between an inferior and a superior, the two actors behave according to the roles assigned to their different statuses. They are necessarily conscious of the ranking of their respective statuses, since their conduct is an expression of the hierarchy. But it is possible for them not to have a clear and explicit view of the total stratification system. In societies where the expressed ideal is egalitarian, but where behaviour conforms to superiority and inferiority roles, collective representations can have an ideological function. They form a screen and prevent one from seeing the system which underlies the behaviour.

This screen did not exist in traditional societies. Collective representations there expressed and approved of inequality. Some mythical tales represented inequality as the consequence of some transgression, others as evidence of different individual abilities. Here is one version of one such tale we have collected in Rwanda. It belongs to the type in which inequality is a punishment. Kazikamuntu, the first man, begot many children, among whom were Gatwa, Gahutu and Gatutsi. Gatwa killed one of his brothers and was cursed for this by his father. The latter, looking for a successor, chose Gahutu to exercise authority over his brothers. Unfortunately, one day when his father had sent him on an important mission, Gahutu had eaten too much and fell asleep. Gatutsi replaced his brother, and acquitted himself very well of his duties. Kazikamuntu then decided that Gatutsi and not Gahutu should succeed him, and be the superior brother. From that time the curse on Gatwa, the punishment of Gahutu and the reward to Gatutsi have been passed on to their descendents, the Twa, Hutu and Tutsi[3].

John Beattie reports from the Bunyoro a story of the inequality-of-abilities type. This mythical tale refers to an Ethiopid dynasty, the Tembuzi, which is said to have preceded the Chwezi, and thus also the invasion of the Nilotic Luo strangers. The first man, Kintu, wanting to give his sons names – until then they had all been called *kana* ('child') – and to choose a successor from among them, put them to two tests. He set down in the path where they were to go six objects: a cow's head, a leather thong, a bowl of millet and sweet potatoes, a grass head ring, an axe, and a knife. The eldest son ate part of the cooked food and took the rest away, balancing the bowl on his head with the help of the head ring; he also took the axe and knife. The second son took the leather thong, and the youngest the cow's head. Then Kintu told his children to sit down and keep a full pot of milk on their knees all night without spilling it. In the morning, only the youngest child still had a full pot. He had actually spilled a little of his milk, but his older brothers had generously given him some of theirs, and the eldest had later spilt all of his. The father decided to call the eldest child, who had chosen the farmer's food and tools and had not been capable of passing the milk test, *Kairu* ('little peasant'). The second child, who had preferred the leather thong, and had not wasted any milk, since he had given some to his brother, he called *Kahuma* ('little herdsman'). The youngest, whose pot had been full, and who had chosen the cow's head, he called *Kakama* ('little king'). Kakama became the first king of the Tembuzi dynasty[4].

Whether the result of a fault, or the confirmation of a difference in ability, inequality was seen as innate and 'natural'. Africans of the traditional period had not, of course, elaborated a theory of heredity versus environment, but the higher ranking individuals at least saw the differences between strata in a light which today we would call 'racist'. In their eyes, the Iru, Hutu and Ha were born lacking the potentiality for certain qualities (lively intelligence, self-control, sense of responsibility, etc.) and could never acquire them. Social inequality simply translated an inequality of nature.

The basis of the hierarchy

The basic hierarchy of the Great Lakes – a superior caste and an inferior class – was obvious, clear-cut and strongly marked. Everyone could place himself and others in that framework. The respective rank of the two actors governed their relationship in all social interaction. What was this very solid and important stratification founded on? What was the basis of the superior's superiority? It is not easy to answer these questions. The solidity of the building contrasts with the fragility of the props supporting it.

Very well-articulated collective representations certainly provide one of the supports of the system: the natural inferiority of the peasants and superiority of the herdsmen, the glorious conquests of fearless warriors, the sudden appearance of innumerable herds of long-horned cattle, and the invincibility of each kingdom's armies in battles with its neighbours. This was the marvellous image of themselves and their past that the Tutsi and Hima created in their oral traditions as they have been collected in the nineteenth and

The colonial era seen through the eyes of a subject. A Yoruba wooden carving representing a European riding a horse. (Museum of Lagos).

twentieth centuries. These conceptions of the origin of the basic inequality of men, these tales of wondrous events, these epic poems, these songs of self-praise, made up a coherent system which, in various forms, both expressed and impressed an idea: the superior caste is the most intelligent, the strongest, the most beautiful and the best. This 'message' was 'diffused' by the arts of the spoken word which, in the Great Lakes region, occupied as important a place in the aesthetic domain as did the visual arts in the societies of the forest and savanna. There can be no doubt that this system of representation provided powerful support to stratification. The structure held because everyone, to a large extent, believed in it.

A second and more materialistic basis of stratification was what seemed to the peasants the advantages of the herdsman in production. Unlike land, which produces crops only in proportion to the work put into it, cattle could provide the herdsman indefinitely with milk, meat and leather, since they continually reproduce themselves. One need only know how to deliver a calf, and where to find pastures in the dry season, and be able to defend them against possible raids. In traditional Africa, where property in land in the Western legal sense did not exist, everyone had easy access to a plot of land, so that obtaining a good harvest was solely a matter of manpower. From this point of view, cattle had the attraction of being 'natural capital'. A herd of cattle, like well-managed capital, increased even if part of the 'interest' was consumed (milk and blood, small bulls and heifers). When unfortunate circumstances such as an exceptionally dry spell, epidemic, locust invasion or the approach of a hostile group, obliged people to move, the peasant had to abandon his planted fields altogether, whereas the herdsman could take his cattle with him.

It is true that in the sedentary kingdoms established several centuries ago in the Great Lake region, the superior caste depended on agricultural rather than pastoral products for its food. George

Murdock estimates this dependence at fifty to sixty per cent in the four societies we are considering here, and this is certainly no exaggeration[5]. It is equally true that the average milk production of a cow was very small, and that cattle-rearing did not aim at producing meat for consumption. Nonetheless, at the end of the traditional period, the cow still retained all its prestige as a noble and highly coveted object of wealth. Only the Tutsi and Hima could own cattle. In Ankole the Iru could not own productive cows. In Rwanda, Burundi and Buha, different restrictions led to practically the same result. This did not, however, prevent the herdsmen from getting help from peasants in tending their cattle, nor entrusting them temporarily with the control of a few. Yet several centuries after the establishment of societies composed of both peasants and herdsmen, descendants of the latter still retained exclusive owner-ship of the means of production which had allowed their ancestors to invade the high plateaux without being tied down by the laborious business of cultivating the land.

The third basis of the superiority of the pastoral caste was its close association with the rulers. All the decision-makers, administra-tors, military leaders and provincial chiefs, besides all the warriors and middle-range officials, were men of superior status. Rulers of course only formed a minority of the caste descended from the herdsmen, which in itself only represented between ten and twenty per cent of the total population. But lineage and caste solidarity created close ties between the Tutsi and Hima rulers and those who, even though they were subjects liable to coercion, enjoyed the same status. The power of coercion, which in all societies sets apart those who possess it and makes them feared, seemed to the peasants in some ways to extend beyond the rulers. Men of the superior caste were subjects, but not in quite the same way as ordinary peasants; this was a confirmation of the latter's inferior status.

Thus the striking superiority of herdsman status rested on three foundations: a system of collective representations, the exclusive ownership of cattle, and the close ties between superiors and rulers. Considered separately, each of these bases seems disproportionate to the combined effect of the three – namely stratification. But it is only by considering them in combination that one can account for the phenomenon.

Power and status

One gets the same feeling of evanescence when one tries to state precisely the relationship between status and power. What power does superior status confer? What goods, what services does it allow one to obtain? Once again, it is impossible to give a direct, simple answer.

The general obligation of the actors in an inequality relationship is to behave according to their respective rank. In the Great Lake societies, the behaviour culturally assigned to an inferior is defined in terms of respect in speech and gesture. He has to agree to everything that is said to him. He expresses his rank by being self-effacing. On the other hand, the superior's role does not give him the right to demand prestations of work or goods, except perhaps small services (taking messages, going to fetch tobacco from a neighbouring settlement, etc.) or occasional gifts (a thirst-quenching jug of beer, a small basket of beans, or a few bananas when needed). The superior cannot apply coercive sanctions. The inferior who does not behave in a suitably respectful way can be reprimanded, ridiculed, or even receive a couple of strokes with a stick. Status *per se* confers no great material advantages.

Of course a warrior herdsman of high prestige could get a good deal out of timid peasants by the mere effect of his rank. But this was only a secondary mechanism. The network of inequality acted as a mediator of power in two other principal ways: superior status

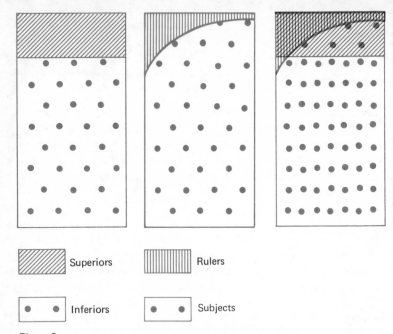

Figure 6
Stratification and government in traditional Rwanda.

made it easier to get into the ruling group; and it allowed those possessing it, in certain societies, to offer protection in return for goods and services.

The herdsman caste constituted the reserve of recruits for the rulers. As we have just mentioned, Tutsi or Hima status was indispensable for entry into most governmental roles. This meant that a young Tutsi or Hima had the possibility (which did not exist for eighty to ninety per cent of the population) of entering the ruling group, that is to say, the political network, which was the support *par excellence* of power relations. That particular way of taking advantage of one's status could obviously only succeed in very few cases.

Protection was institutionalised in the networks of feudal dependence, *okutoisha*, *ubuhake*, and *ubugabire*, which will be discussed in the next chapter. We simply want to show here the kind of conditions that made this protection almost indispensable for men of lower status. In theory, the inferior who behaved in a way befitting his rank, treating men of the pastoral caste with respect, should have been able to avoid trouble and to have no need of a protector. Unfortunately, the close ties between superiors and rulers gave the superiors indirect ways of applying pressure on individual peasants. Proverbs attest to the universal truth that a big man can always find ways of causing a little man trouble when he wants to. The attentive ear lent by the rulers to the complaints of a member of their caste against one of his peasant neighbours guaranteed that the poor farmer would be in for a series of harassments and perhaps serious difficulties. If a man of pastoral status denounced a peasant's actions, the judge simply took his word for it; but if a peasant complained about a herdsman, he had to prove to a judge of herdsman status that he had grounds for complaint. The injured farmer was better off letting matters go, even if he had been the victim of some serious damage.

This *de facto* immunity assured by caste solidarity allowed any superior to apply strong pressures on any inferior. It is on the fear of this possibility that rests the power inherent in superior status. It was so much dreaded (although it was not continually applied) that a peasant had to obtain the protection of a superior to try to some extent to re-establish a balance of power. Thus if he was threatened by another man of superior status, he could counter him with a man of equal status willing to act on his behalf. This protection was paid for with goods and services.

After this long exposition, we finally see how in some of the interlacustrine societies, membership of the superior caste was translated into power. The immunity enjoyed by the superiors led them to apply pressure on the inferiors, who, in order to defend themselves individually, would 'pay' for a superior's protection.

But this is not the end of the story. We shall see that this protection was not left to individual initiative, but was organised into feudal institutions[6].

Upset equilibrium in traditional stratification

The model of the network of inequality we have just described was maintained, during the traditional period, by a balance of opposing forces: inferiors seeking change, and superiors defending their privileges and trying to extend them. But, unlike what happened in the traditional political field, the point of equilibrium was reached at a high level of tension. Since all the historical traditions that we know come from the superior caste, they say nothing of the peasants' discontent. We can only infer this from the few clues we have. There was a popular oral tradition of savagely cynical stories and proverbs directed against the superior caste which circulated underground. It paralleled the aristocratic tradition which glorified the nobles and justified inequality. One or two movements of opposition to the network of stratification appeared at the beginning of the German conquest of East Africa. It is very likely that they were not the first of their kind, but that the memory of others has been carefully suppressed in historical traditions. The first elections in 1956 in Rwanda and Burundi showed, when analysed, an important 'spontaneous' division between the strata. The violence of the Hutu revolution in November 1959 can only be explained by a caste hatred that goes far back into pre-colonial times[7]. Where the inequality model persisted at the end of the pre-colonial period, it was based on an equilibrium which the superiors constantly re-established, and on certain institutions – the network of feudal dependence, for example – which reduced the tension by breaking up the horizontal divisions of stratification.

Colonial rule did not upset the equilibrium at all. Being political in nature, it obviously destroyed traditional political networks, as we saw above. But it allowed the old stratifications to remain. They were no obstacle to its hold on Africans, and they even met with complicity from colonial governors and administrators who, as was only natural, welcomed a hierarchical and ordered society. Besides, they themselves established one based on the same model, as we shall see.

Colonial rule, however, gave rise, as the years passed, to new differences among the African population. The most important was that which singled out from the mass those who had received a western-type education. This was a group of literate people known in the language of the British colonies as 'educated Africans' or in the French colonial jargon as 'les évolués'. The amount of education varied. A spoken and written knowledge of the colonial language was the first step. Beyond this, specialist occupations were common: typist, secretary, accountant, mechanic, electrician, cabinet-maker, etc. In other professions such as medicine, agronomy, veterinary medicine and administration the first stages were separated from the complete training so that there were assistant administrators, medical aides, etc. Finally, particularly during the last decade before independence, Africans completed university courses. Other criteria besides education created new categories among the African population of the colonies. In the Gold Coast (the colony which, when it became independent, called itself Ghana) and the Ivory Coast, Africans became plantation owners. In Kampala, Brazzaville and Léopoldville (now Kinshasa) African trades and businesses were set up and developed. Education, however, still seemed to be the most basic and general phenomenon of differentiation in colonial Black Africa.

In societies where there was a traditional hereditary stratification which assigned a status to everyone, and regulated access to privileged goods, a new privileged group emerged based on some-

162

thing hitherto unknown: book learning. For some time writing did not change the balance of forces in the field of inequality. According to the stratum from which the educated men came, they lent their weight to superiors or inferiors. Thus in Rwanda, after some hesitation, the Tutsi adopted the new basis of social influence, education, and tried to keep it exclusively to themselves. To some extent they succeeded, as is shown by the proportion of Tutsi among the Rwanda Catholic clergy, among office employees and assistants in many professions. Although the Tutsi only represented at most twenty per cent of the total population, they made up two-thirds or three-quarters of the literates.

Meanwhile, even in the best conditions for the maintenance of the old hierarchy, the irruption of the educated class eventually upset the internal equilibrium of the inequality model. The literate among the superior caste, who now had a new means of social promotion at their disposal, were rarely champions of the old social order; and the literate group emerging from the lower strata were less and less willing to adopt the deferential behaviour appropriate to their roles. They had other effective weapons besides: western ideas of equality to oppose to the ideologies of superior strata, and the individual security that professional skill ensured them. Independently of the actions of the revolutionary literates, one must add that new commercial circuits, monetary incomes, and the extension of the global society to the whole colony defined a new social situation, incompatible with the retention of the old hierarchy. We emphasise the importance of the literate group, because they were actually part of the field of forces which a dynamic model is.

The equilibrium of the traditional network of inequality had always been the result of a high tension between two opposing forces. To the increasing pressure of the inferiors (increasing because the bases of superiority were more and more often quest-

ioned in the colonial context) was added the impatience of their
educated members. The traditional aristocratic caste was no longer
in a position to re-establish equilibrium once more by increasing its
force. It tried to do so in Rwanda by violence. This was a desperate
venture which ruined them. Before the end of the colonial period
(1962 for Rwanda) the superior caste of Tutsi no longer existed.
Elsewhere, the traditional stratification survived locally in some
distant villages, or in particularly conservative spheres such as those
of matrimonial alliance. A secretary's family, for example, would
sometimes refuse her permission to marry a minister, because he
came from a traditionally lower stratum.

The colonial networks of inequality

While the traditional stratification was fading away or rapidly
collapsing, societies stemming from colonisation were creating a
new network of inequality. It was new in that it did not continue
its predecessors and was established even where traditional
societies had been homogeneous; but it also somewhat resembled
the old in that it was 'constructed' on the same model.

Within the framework of each colonial territory, society as a whole
was divided into two distinct groups: whites and natives. Contrary to
certain assertions current in official circles at the end of the colonial
period, these two groups were not juxtaposed, living parallel, but
superimposed and hierarchical. There was, in fact, constant interaction between the two groups, and it was obvious that in these
interactions a white and a native did not behave as equals. If the perfectly neutral word 'native' has gradually acquired a pejorative
meaning, and even become an insult, it is because it expressed an inferior status. Here we use it in its primary sense of 'born in the
country'.

The upper stratum consisted of nationals of the metropolitan

country, of other countries in Europe and North America, and all those who were socially considered whites (which would exclude certain Caucasoids such as Arabs and Indians). When they were sufficiently numerous, these Asiatics formed a separate stratum ranking between the whites and the natives; when there were only a few ɹ ey were assimilated to superiors or inferiors according to their way of life. The lower stratum comprised the colony's African inhabitants, and other Africans considered socially as members of the black race. Mulattos, male and female (always thought to have sprung from a white father and African mother) had the status of the milieu in which they were raised, European or African. In some colonies the legislation gave a child who was recognised the right to maintenance from his father. But this made no difference to his subsequent status, which depended solely upon where he had grown up.

Within each of these strata there were numerous levels based on differences of occupation, wealth, education, etc. But each level did not constitute a stratum with a culturally defined status. The director of a mining company, a school accountant or shop-owner, among themselves were equal; they went to the same restaurants, their children went to the same schools and could marry each other. In their relations with a black, whoever he was, they were superior.

Colonial strata were endogamous; the few exceptions to this rule appeared only at the end of the colonial régime, and usually in a non-colonial society. A typical example was the African who studied in Europe, and there married a European girl who had never lived in a colony. In many colonies the law made marriage between persons of different strata difficult, since whites were subject to the written law of the metropolis, and the blacks to various kinds of customary law.

To a great extent, the occupations of members of each stratum were different. Manual labour and menial office jobs were native occupations; in every field whites filled all the directory and supervisory posts and did the work which required higher or intermediate qualifications. It was rare to find identical positions occupied indiscriminately by blacks and whites. There were 'black jobs' and 'white jobs' even if the line separating them was not everywhere in the same place.

Segregation, as far as was compatible with the demands of business or factory and commercial or industrial profit, was established everywhere. It was most noticeable in recreation and social life; sports and games, receptions and clubs, theatre performances and lectures, were designed either for black or for white. All contact was avoided; hospitals, hostels, restaurants, railways and boats all had places or compartments reserved for superiors, or even, when it was possible, entirely separate buildings at a distance from one another (a school for whites, a school for blacks; a maternity ward for whites and one for blacks, etc.). Neither did they lived in the same neighbourhood. Colonial town-planners had made provision for segregation in their blueprints. When we look at this today, it seems strange. In the centre of town were government and business districts: this was a small area and besides containing the head offices of industrial and commercial organisations, it had banks, luxury shops, restaurants, a few bars and night clubs. Around this, in the best laid out and most salubrious areas, the vast residential quarters for Europeans; each villa was surrounded by a garden where one lived amidst lawns, flowers and shrubs. Further on, one finds the black quarter with innumerable little houses crowded in the rectangles formed by wide streets with neither tree nor asphalt. For most urban whites whose business did not compel them to go into these 'native cities', and for all their wives and children, these native cities were urban excrescences, unfamiliar and somewhat frightening. Yet these were African towns.

Colonial residential patterns: segregated and unequal. *Left* White residential district in Durban, South Africa; *below* shacks provided for black mine workers in Rhodesia.

Such separate material frameworks of life were obviously unequal. On the one side there was comfort, space and luxury; on the other constriction, jostling and poverty. The standards of life in these different surroundings were far apart. Consumer goods, household equipment and clothes differed greatly both in quantity and quality in the two strata. The superior stratum sought to justify the difference by asserting that there were two contrasting cultural traditions rather than two actual levels; that, for example, the costly food imported by the whites was not appreciated by the blacks. And some housewife could always be found to say that her cook never tasted the sauces he prepared, and that he personally preferred traditional food.

That each stratum had its own cultural heritage is certain. But the common heritage of all members of a traditional society was only maintained (and even then imperfectly) in villages. For a man living mainly on wages, married or living with a woman who often came from another traditional society, the ancestral culture was full of gaps. It was certainly no obstacle to appreciating all that money could buy. There may be minority cultures of ascetics indifferent to material wealth, but such subcultures certainly did not exist in traditional Black Africa, where wealth has always been prized. The blacks saw the European standard of living as a better and an enviable one, even if they had not learned to appreciate caviare, oysters and escargots à la bourguignonne!

One belonged to the higher stratum either by being born of parents who belonged to it, or by having a father in it who provided an education in a white milieu, or by coming to live in the colony and being considered there as one of the white race. In addition some colonial legislation granted the legal status of European to certain natives, individually or in categories. Those so privileged enjoyed the same rights as the whites (the right to contract a loan, for example, in colonies where it was otherwise forbidden to natives), but it was very rare for them to be able to cross the barriers of social segregation. Because of these separate and closed characteristics, the superior stratum was a caste. And the same was true of the lower stratum. Unlike the man of superior status in the traditional stratification, a white who could not maintain his rank, and whose way of life approached that of the lower stratum, could not lose himself in the same way that a herdsman could merge into the peasant class and become an Iru or Hutu. Because it was justified in terms of race, colonial inequality was translated into closed separate divisions, that is, into castes.

Some European and Indian shopkeepers
catered for the African market.
Goods in their shops were likely
to be sold at high prices.

Collective representations of colonial inequality

The superior privileged white caste had elaborated collective representations explaining stratification and justifying the advantages of their own status.

Like the Hima and the Tutsi – probably like all aristocrats – the whites were convinced of their own great worth. This conviction was translated into simplified stereotypes which contrasted the white's sense of responsibility, his clear perception of effective action, single mindedness and logical intelligence with the black's lazy irresponsibility, lack of the power to think ahead and organise, fickleness and inability to see beyond the concrete. Thanks to this extraordinary combination of qualities, Europeans had created Western civilisation, and led the world in scientific and philosophical thought and technical achievements; while the blacks had invented practically nothing, having stayed at a primitive level of life with infantile ideas.

These stereotypes, which were very widespread among the superior colonial caste, rested on two doctrines which were not clearly distinguished: that which affirms a hierarchy of cultures and that which affirms a hierarchy of races. The first, which is logically independent of the second, maintains that social heritages – cultures – including religions, forms of marriage, political systems, etc. can be ranked in an absolute order. There is one culture which is the best, and in colonial eyes this was the entity vaguely described as 'western civilisation'. The doctrine of the superiority of western civilisation does not actually condemn those of the lower cultures to be forever deprived of this highest of all civilisations. The process of apprenticeship might be lengthy, but it was possible. As the colonial whites were fond of repeating. 'It took us two thousand years to get where we are. The blacks can't catch up in two or three generations'.

In contrast, the doctrine of racial superiority refers to an inborn, and thus unalterable, superiority. The 'white race' are endowed with hereditary traits common to them all and exclusive to them, which assure them a superior mental development to that of other 'races'. The blacks' potential is limited forever by their genetic heritage. This concept is basically identical to that of the inequality-of-abilities which has such an important place in the mental representations of the traditional higher castes. It has the same ideological function: to justify the privileges of a minority by an argument which assures their perpetuation because it finds their roots in biology.

We have not examined the merits of the traditional ideologies, nor shall we do this for the colonial ones. In spite of their scientific pretensions (after all, the evaluation of cultures belongs to comparative anthropology, and the evaluation of genetical potentiality to human biology), cultural and racial superiority were dogmas of as fragile a substance as the story of the father of all men cursing one of his sons and condemning him (and all his descendants) to be slaves to his other sons (and all their descendants).

The words and conduct of the whites were far from forming a coherent whole. First, the two fundamental dogmas were partly contradictory. It was quite common, however, to hear a person say in the same breath that 'the blacks are congenitally inferior to us' and that 'if we let them into our universities they will soon catch up with us'. The key concept of 'race' sometimes meant a narrow group which in fact was distinguished only by cultural characteristics (the 'Luba race', for instance), at other times populations who had nothing in common but the fact that they spoke related languages (the 'Bantu race', for example), and then sometimes simply dark-skinned people all over the world. The superior caste set great store by racial purity, but whites who had black concubines and mulatto children did not incur public disapproval. On the other hand, a white woman with a black lover would arouse first sheer incredulity, and then the strongest and most sincere condemnation. In the white collective imagination, the black man was moved by violent impulses, and endowed with incomparable sexual potency and a genital organ of exceptional size. But in their everyday and domestic relationships with white women blacks were expected to behave in a more sexless manner than whites.

These inconsistencies well demonstrate that racism is a secondary phenomenon in relation to stratification. It is not the basis of inequality – as its protagonists would have us believe – but its result. The ambiguous and emotional realm of sex is very revealing. It was not purity of race that mattered, but the tacit evidence of superiority of status which allowed white men access to black women, but denied white women to black men; which authorised a type of familiarity that subtly denied black masculinity. Colonial superiority did not reflect a belief in a natural inequality; on the contrary, the racist doctrine was a superstructure arising from an advantageous network of societal inequality.

Power mechanisms of the superior colonial caste

Superior status *per se* did not confer rights over the goods and services of inferiors. The role of the latter was limited to recognising by their behaviour to whites that they were of inferior status. This behaviour gave those who benefited from it the moral satisfaction of pre-eminence and of being treated with deference. But precedence is not power.

A more appreciable advantage was exclusive access to certain remunerative activities for which one had to have full legal responsibility. The laws against giving credit, the restrictions on acquiring certain kinds of property, the prohibition of 'dangerous' activities such as the traffic in spirits, were originally measures 'for the protection of natives'. But as time passed, they became more of a hindrance than a help, and, in fact, favoured the whites by protecting them from competition.

Caste solidarity clearly came into play, and had its usual effects. By belonging to the same closed minority as the rulers, the whites got from them all they had a right to, and sometimes a little more. In case of conflict between a superior and an inferior, the former's arguments were examined attentively and sympathetically. When a white broke the law, it was not unusual for him to get a lighter sentence from colonial judges than he would from their metropolitan counterparts. This meant that whites could, by skilful manoeuvring, exert considerable pressure on individuals or groups belonging to the inferior caste.

Precedence, specially reserved activities, links with rulers by virtue of caste (all of which existed in traditional stratifications too) do not complete the picture of colonial inequality. One must add that the colonies, although they were distinct societies, were not completely cut off from the metropolis. Their ties with the latter had a special bearing on the power of the superior caste (which they increased) and on the pressures to which the native population was subjected (which they reduced).

We have already mentioned the unique economic system in which metropolis and colony constituted two complementary parts. It was through the intermediacy of this system that the superior caste turned its status to material advantage. This system made the principal material advantages of white status impersonal and indirect. Mining and industrial enterprises and the great commercial plantations were more profitable in the colonies than similar enterprises in Europe because of the abundance of raw materials, the climatic conditions and cheap native labour. Part of these higher profits was interest on capital invested, and part provided high wages for the European personnel, with numerous fringe benefits (free accommodation in furnished lodgings belonging to the employer, medical care, various perquisites, holidays in the home country, free travel, etc.). High pay and fringe benefits allowed Europeans to attain the high standards of living characteristic of their caste. These advantages were not obtained directly from the native majority, but resulted from the colonial economic circuit. The white personnel of the large enterprises were not the only ones to benefit materially. The specialised services of colonial administration (medicine, geology, agronomy, etc.), the institutions of learning, and other public and private institutions, paid their staff at rates close to those of the industrial companies. There too the advantages of white status were obtained through taxation (paid by all subjects) on the one hand, and on the other by wages and salaries paid by the public treasury either directly (to officials and such like) or indirectly, by subsidies to institutions of teaching and research.

Only a complex economic analysis which would be difficult to make would permit one to calculate how much the superior stratum obtained from the inferior stratum beyond the services it rendered. This margin would be the measure of their power. Even without this kind of calculation (which will doubtless never be attempted), we can get some idea from the following facts: at the end of the colonial period, the white castes flourished in all the colonies, and all the colonies were underdeveloped in the sense that the black castes had a lower standard of living than the average population of industrial countries (those in which less than 50 per cent of the population are engaged in agriculture).

In spite of the great *de facto* autonomy granted to the governor and his administration, the colony was politically tied to the organs of government of the metropolis. Parliamentarians were sensitive to press campaigns, movements of public opinion and the positions taken up by the parties, and they reacted when pressure was exercised by the superior caste on the blacks to a degree that they

considered abusive. Of course all the abuses of power that superior
status makes possible did not become known at home and were not
publicly discussed. But the fear of scandal that was felt as much by
the administration as by private enterprise constituted some kind of
guarantee for the blacks. When Rhodesia in 1965 cut its political
ties with the United Kingdom, while at the same time maintaining
its network of stratification, the absence of this brake was immediately felt. The whites derived more advantages from their status
than they ever had before.

From colonial inequality to stratification
in independent Africa

As long as the two opposing forces of superiors and inferiors were
in equilibrium, the inequality network corresponding to the
colonial model we have just analysed continued to exist. The

combination of pressure from within the network (from the group of educated Africans) and an external event (political independence) deeply disturbed this equilibrium, but the model changed less than one might have expected.

At the beginning of the fifties, there was an increase in the number of literate Africans within the black caste in which the traditional stratification was fading out. They had acquired more skills and better qualifications. The demarcation line between castes had two consequences which they would not accept: it prevented some of them from getting jobs for which they had the necessary qualifications simply because these were 'for whites'; it was an obstacle to equality of pay for blacks in posts almost identical with those of whites. Their wages were lower (because, so it was said, they were not expatriates like the Europeans); so were the fringe benefits (because, so it was said, the blacks did not have the same needs). The liberalisation of the colonial political régime which had cautiously developed during these years allowed the formation of professional associations and trade unions, and the public airing of grievances. The pressure applied by the educated blacks thus added considerably to the weight of the large inferior stratum.

Political independence deprived the superior caste of their close ties with the rulers. White colonial rulers, of the same nationality as most members of the superior caste and sharing their cultural heritage, gave way to the rulers of the independent states, who had led the anti-colonial fight, denounced racial inequality and were black. The superiors could no longer count on the complicity of the rulers, nor could they any longer justify their privileges by the ideology of racial superiority.

After an uncertain transition period, however, one could see that stratification had not been swept away in the wake of political independence. As the barrier which had prevented the advancement of educated people was now lifted, they took up positions which until then had been reserved for whites. There were many vacant positions in public administration; many colonial officials were obliged or chose to return to Europe, and to continue their careers in administration there. Where independence went hand in hand with trouble, as in Congo-Léopoldville (today Kinshasa) – the number of officials who left assumed the proportions of an exodus; in a few weeks the administrative pyramid was depleted of European officials. Private enterprises began, for obvious reasons, what was called 'Africanising the staff'. This promotion of educated Africans changed the personnel but not the organisation.

The diagrams of office organisation remained the same (the definition of professional roles, office head, assistant director, director, etc., did not change). Nor did the material structures (private houses whose relative importance corresponded to the occupier's position in the job hierarchy, luxurious residential quarters, clubs and swimming pools).

Men with high or medium positions in public institutions and private enterprises, enjoying good pay and a higher standard of living than the peasant masses, constitute the nucleus of a new stratum. They have sometimes been called the 'bourgeoisie'. If, with European history in mind, we mean by this a class of industrial or commercial entrepreneurs, the term is hardly applicable to the social group we are trying to describe. It includes very few who get their incomes from business (plantations, shops, work-shops, etc.) and even fewer who draw income from investments.

One can identify a social stratification undergoing formation in the still very fluid situation of the global societies of independent Africa. The higher stratum includes, besides the directors and managerial personnel of public administration and private companies and the owners of the small businesses we have just mentioned, foremen, technicians and skilled workers, as well as teachers in primary, secondary and higher education. They have in

In independent Africa, hospital facilities are available almost exclusively to city dwellers.

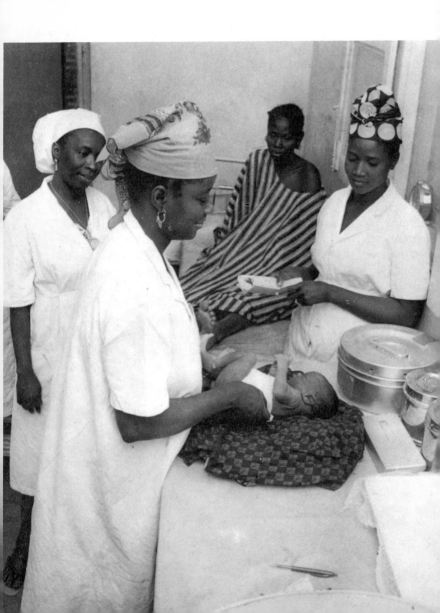

common a relatively high level of education, which gives them the necessary skills for their specialised jobs, a monetary income which enables them to live without working the land, a 'modern' style of life (where clothes, food, housing and the language in daily use differ greatly from traditional norms) and, lastly, residence in towns.

This last feature can be explained by an important fact about contemporary Africa: only the town (often only the capital) offers the superior stratum the kind of living conditions they want. The jobs we have just listed are rarely found outside the most important urban centres. 'Modern' leisure activities, cafés and restaurants, orchestras and dancing, libraries and newspapers, sports grounds and cinemas, are by-products of city life. The only means of entering the superior stratum are to be found in the town: the best secondary schools, specialist training and advanced studies. Also, which is no less important, there one finds the social and professional connections which lead to promotion, appointment to a job, or obtaining a grant to study abroad.

This upper stratum undoubtedly constitutes a class. It is not hereditary; a peasant's son, if he has completed the necessary studies, can enter it. It is not exclusive; common descent ties continue to unite successful city-dwellers with their relatives in the villages. One sees, however, the first signs of stabilisation. Those at the summit of the urban class try to make sure that their children will also stay there; they send them to the best schools, and encourage marriages between young people with the same background.

Not all town-dwellers are educated and prosperous. An urban proletariat was formed during the colonial period. The extraordinary growth of town populations during the colonial period (the norm and not the exception was for them to multiply fifteen to twenty times in thirty to forty years[8]) is due to the massive influx of young peasants with little or no education hoping to find well-paid work and a less monotonous existence in the towns than in the villages. For some of them (depending on economic circumstances) work was frequently intermittent and earnings poor. Independence did not change this movement. The town still has its attractions. Social advancement is possible only in town. City dwellers are characterised, regardless of their position, by the value they place on success, and by the way in which they conceive of it.

The second class is the peasant mass, who are very numerous. Using the findings of experts in the African Council of Science which met in Abidjan in 1961, one can estimate it at about 90 per cent of the total population. From figures collected between 1956 and 1959 in the French colonies, one can calculate that 88 per cent of the total population lived by agriculture[9]. Peasants really constitute a lower class. They are just as isolated as under colonialism, perhaps even more so. Social services (medical, educational, economic) are more and more concentrated in the capital. Foreign aid arrives in the capital and seems often not to go any further.

The gap between city and country dwellers widens. Two different subcultures are appearing; modes of behaviour expressing inequality emerge; the condescending attitude of the city dwellers is matched by the resentment of country dwellers. We can witness the formation of a new network of inequality, characteristic of independent Africa.

But the former superior white caste did not disappear with the end of the colonial governments. In some young states its numbers have diminished, in others they seem to have increased. It fits into the new network of inequality: in the urban class, at the top. It takes part in the system but retains its own identity, like a subgroup in a whole. Old and new superiors both have the same status in professional relationships. They are equals and behave as such. But in social relationships, integration is not advancing significantly,

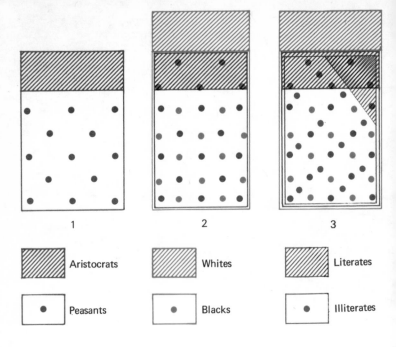

| 1 | 2 | 3 |

| ▨ Aristocrats | ▨ Whites | ▨ Literates |
| ▫ Peasants | ▫ Blacks | ▫ Illiterates |

partly because of memories of a racist ideology which has outlived the circumstances that produced it, and partly because of the usual reaction of an 'old aristocracy' to 'upstarts'. There is, too, an attitude of extreme reserve on the part of the Africans. They also remember the racist ideology, but, more important than that, they know that the whites, even directors of big companies, are foreigners in transit, and solidarity with their own class and ties with the rulers are more important than joining in the amusements of the whites.

From the point of view of the peasant class, the whites remain what they have always been, superiors. Just as before, under colonisation, they all (including the agents of technical co-operation working in the villages) have an incomparably higher standard of living than the farmers, the power of knowledge, personal relations with rulers, and are not tied down to monotonous dreary work. They never stay long.

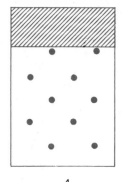

4

Town-dwellers

Villagers

The functions of inequality

The three models of inequality which have followed one another in
less than a century in sub-Saharan Africa have been identified by
their formal characteristics: two or three hierarchical statuses
attributed to all the members of a global society, which determine
the behaviour of superiority/inferiority or equality in the relations
between them. What is the use of a network of inequality in a
social system?

In the traditional societies of the Great Lakes, its function was to
perpetuate an event: the conquest that had taken place at a precise
moment in history in a certain place on the high plateaux. The
herdsmen conquered the cultivators because they were stronger (by
virtue of their arms) and richer (by virtue of their production
techniques in cattle herding). This localised supremacy was
essentially temporary. Because they were not merely passing

The colonial stratification perpetuated the European military superiority at the time of the conquest. Shown here, a mountain train returning from a British military expedition in the nineteenth century.

through, but actually settled down peacefully, and because of their constant interaction with the cultivators, the herdsmen could have formed a homogeneous society (where everyone could cultivate the land, raise cattle, marry whomsoever he wanted, and take part in any festivity); or they could have formed a society that was specialised in a parallel direction (where different occupational groups exchanged products for other goods). These two hypotheses are not mere conjecture. In the Kingdom of Buganda and the Soga chiefdoms (situated in the cultural area of the Great Lakes and formed by pastors of Luo origin) the societies as they existed in the nineteenth century were homogeneous. There were differences in occupation and wealth between individuals, families or lineages, but they had nothing to do with strata. On the other hand, Nkole oral traditions mention a distant period in the past when Hima pastors and Iru agriculturalists exchanged meat and milk in return for sorghum and beans[10]. It is very possible that this Golden Age is a product of Iru imagination, rather than actual history. Yet a society with specialised but non-hierarchical groups is, to say the least, a collective representation of the inferiors.

But whatever the alternatives might have been, the victorious invaders chose, in the societies discussed earlier, to perpetuate their conquest by passing on to their descendants the advantages of a situation which was essentially temporary. Their descendants made themselves into a separate, closed caste which reserved to itself the exclusive right to the invaders' instruments of supremacy, namely the use of arms and the ownership of cattle.

We find the same function of perpetuating momentary supremacy when we analyse colonial stratification. Military expeditions in nineetenth-century Black Africa succeeded for the same reasons. The Europeans were stronger (by virtue of their arms) and richer (by virtue of their techniques of industrial production). They too took up residence and formed new global societies which might

have been of another kind. But, unlike the traditional invasions, colonisation was a national project and not based on clan or lineage. They kept the advantages of conquest to pass them on to the compatriots of the explorers and soldiers rather than to their own descendants. White colonial castes were composed largely of nationals of the metropolitan country, and not of the offspring of the first conquerors.

A closed and segregated caste is formed in order to retain the economic privileges of the initial occupation for the citizens of the colonial metropolis (remunerative employment, highly profitable investments, protected markets, cheap raw materials, etc.). The native caste was totally deprived of one of the instruments of conquest: arms. But it did have access to the other: industrial techniques, through education and the money economy. As we have seen, the effect of their participation in these two sources of modernity was to increase the pressure from the inferior caste and thus upset the equilibrium of the colonial network of inequality.

It is too soon to know whether stratification into two classes in independent Africa will also have as its prime function the perpetuation of another transitory situation: the promotion of the educated Africans at the moment of political independence.

A second function of African stratification is to maintain and reinforce the political network. Herdsman caste, white caste and urban caste are all composed of subjects. But these subjects are very close to the rulers. If they can put pressure on persons of lower status it is because solidarity within their stratum assures them the rulers' support in the event of conflict with an inferior, and impunity for discreet minor breaches of law. The upper stratum constitutes, moreover, the ranks from which the rulers are recruited. For an ambitious man this is actually the biggest advantage of superior status – easy access to governmental roles. Under these conditions, conflicts between rulers and superiors can only be superficial or incidental. They both benefit from the same social order. Though their basic interests may differ, they cannot be antagonistic. The disappearance of traditional rulers at the end of the nineteenth century, and of colonial rulers seventy-five years later, throws light on the connexion between the political and inequality networks. In both cases, stratification survived political downfall, sometimes for a long time. Finally, the traditional superior caste faded away, without having established close ties either with the colonial or the independent rulers. The white caste survives now in contemporary Africa only to the extent that it can establish close ties with the new African rulers.

These are the two functions of some African networks of inequality which analysis brings to light: to fix for several generations the historical situation in which one group dominates another; and to strengthen the political network which itself supports the superior stratum, as an essential part of the whole social order. We can see no other functions. From the analogy between a society and a living organism, it has been argued that the different groups in a society must necessarily be subordinate to one another, as are the parts of the human body, so that the whole can function smoothly. That social activities must be organised in a complementary manner, and that occupations must be specialised and varied are sociological truisms. But it does not follow that each activity must have a corresponding status, that these statuses must be ranked, and that the actors must express their rank by behaviour expressing inferiority/superiority. African systems of stratification have essentially only two levels and this does not correspond to complementary social activities of which there are many more. Moreover, as historical and mythical Nkole tales show, diversity of occupation is indeed compatible with equality of actors.

From an examination of our three African models of inequality, we can also conclude that a relation of superiority is not necessarily a relation of power. The role of superior does not include the right to exact goods and services without an economic return (as does the role of ruler). One 'cashes in' on one's status only indirectly; one puts pressure on inferiors by intimidation and threats until one gets what one wants out of them. This process involves the passive or active complicity of some of the rulers. In the next chapter we will see a particularly neat traditional solution to this problem.

Outside observers' descriptions of stratification (anthropological or sociological) often give the impression that all strata of the same network are organised in exactly the same way; if one is closed, all are closed; if one is endogamous, they all are. When one studies the origin of any stratification – as we have tried to do here – one sees that it starts with a small group which affirms its superiority, emphasising whatever differentiates it from the others, and excluding individuals which it does not recognise as its own kind. It is this group which forces the others to consider themselves as one or more inferior strata. If these inferior strata eventually also develop an *esprit de corps*, an exclusive subculture, and a closed character, it is by way of response, or as a reaction to the superiors.

8 Dependence relations

Dependence is universal. Every natural or manufactured article, every living entity and every action is dependent upon something, and conditioned by things outside itself. One has to really strain the imagination to find an example of something independent. One could perhaps say that the total sum of what exists is not dependent, since there is nothing outside it. Or one can think of the First Cause as it was conceived in Aristotelian tradition. Certainly one has to look a long way to find something that is not dependent.

It is true that here we are only interested in the relation of dependence between men. In the preceding paragraph, we have mentioned the general meaning of the term as used by philosophers, in order better to understand interpersonal dependence. Being dependent on someone means that one cannot fulfil oneself without the intervention of that person. 'To fulfil oneself' is a vague concept, but it means that the dependent needs the other person in vital areas: to live, to develop, to make full use of his powers. This does not include many relationships with people whose co-operation is necessary only in a very restricted field. For example, I need a bookseller to buy books, and an innkeeper for lodging, but I am not for that reason dependent upon them.

A diffuse dependence is present in many human relationships. Just as relations which are not primarily those of power often have an element of power in them, many types of interpersonal and societal relations contain an element of dependence. Among those relationships which do not fit into any exact cultural schema and are largely a matter of improvisation (those we call interpersonal) are friendship and love, which generally have a large element of dependence and even of reciprocal dependence. Friends and lovers often need one another to fulfil themselves. The relationship between a young child and an adult entrusted with the task of teaching him will nearly always be tinged with dependence. Societal relations (those joining actors with culturally defined roles in a

A Tutsi *shebuja* (lord) in Rwanda tasting
the milk offered to him as a regular
tribute by one of his Hutu vassals (*garagu*).

global society) can also sustain diffuse dependence. In a kinship
network, the young lineage member and his patriarch; in marriage,
the husband and his wife; in government, the official and his
minister, all have roles which include a certain amount of
dependence.

Some have gone further, and said that if dependence feelings and
behaviour are obviously not included in the roles of ruler and
superior, yet these actors still exist only by reference to other
actors, the subjects and inferiors. A king without subjects is no
longer a king, and a nobleman without commoners is no longer a
nobleman. This last argument belongs to logic rather than to
anthropology: having defined actors only in terms of a relationship, when we do away with this relationship the actors disappear
along with it. This may be true, but it does not tell us much about
dependence.

The relation of dependence

The idea of diffuse dependence which colours other relations is not
a very useful concept in our research, which seeks to delimit networks that re-group and organise societal relations, corresponding
to certain irreducible types. But if we can isolate an elementary
relation of dependence of this irreducible type, we shall have a
very useful concept which will enable us to recognise a new network
in different societies, and compare the different embodiment of
this network.

Dependence, this need for the help of others in order to live
fully, dominates certain recognised, even institutionalised relations
in many societies. Because of this prevalent aspect, let us call them
relations of dependence. They are asymmetrical; one side gives help
and support; the other receives them and renders various services
to his protector in other ways. The relationship cannot be inverted;

protection and services rendered are not of the same order. The dependent cannot provide his protector with help analogous to what he receives from him; for the protector to give his dependent the same kind of services the latter provides him with would make no sense.

It may be said that the protector has a psychological need for dependents in order to fulfil himself, and this is no doubt right, but that does not change the relationship. Motivation, conscious or not, is not the concern of a study of societal or inter-personal relations. Whether one wishes to become a ruler for monetary gain, to satisfy the need to dominate, to serve one's party, or to compensate for sexual impotence, has no bearing on the political relationship. The same is true of the relation of dependence.

The protector must have the means to fulfil his role. This means that even before embarking upon the relationship, he must be more, or have more, than his potential dependent. This difference may be the future protector's superiority of status, or his membership of a ruling group, his greater wealth, a higher position in a professional hierarchy (which generally means that he controls employment at lower levels), greater reputation (a celebrity with many society connexions wields great influence), or simply by the command of greater physical force, which can be very important in times of trouble. The dependent necessarily having fewer means, generally much fewer, can only render very small services; he can do manual work for his protector, run errands, serve in guarding his house, join in his entourage (thus demonstrating his prestige) help him in his professional activities.

An essential characteristic of the dependence relationship is that protector and dependent choose one another for their individual qualities. This characteristic distinguishes this relationship from all the others we have hitherto encountered. With the exception of matrimonial alliance (that is, for the spouses, not, naturally, for the other affines) all the networks impose upon each actor all the others. That is, one chooses neither one's parents, descendants, king, subjects, superiors, equals nor inferiors. But one does choose one's protector. A protector does not usually take the first step and offer his protection, but he must always either accept or reject the prospective dependent. Of course, a situation can arise in which there is only one person to whom a man can turn for help. This can happen in marriage, too, but in both cases the principle of choice remains. It sometimes happens, too, that a dependence relation becomes hereditary; when a dependent dies, his son succeeds him as dependent of the same protector; the same thing happens when a protector disappears. But even there, a vestige of choice remains. The two heirs must confirm (and may refuse to do so), the continuance of the tie which bound their predecessors.

This initial choice gives the ensuing relationship a personal quality, one which kindles trust, even friendship. Two men choose each other because they consider one another reliable. The atmosphere that is established is thus very different from that of relations where actors are assigned to one. Mutual trust explains at least in part why it is difficult to enumerate the rights and obligations of the reciprocal roles with any precision. Even where they are culturally defined, the roles seem to fall short of the actual behaviour. One could say that explicit roles indicate the manifest aim of a relationship as it is seen by members of a society but that, besides this, the dependent everywhere can always appeal to the protector when he is in trouble, and the protector can ask of him any kind of exceptional service.

Clientship and feudality

The relation of dependence, whose essential characteristics we have just outlined, usually takes two forms, or two models which it is useful to contrast: clientship and feudality. To simplify the description, we shall call the two actors in the relation of feudal dependence by the usual terms of lord and vassal, and those in the clientship relation by the terms patron and client. The terms protector and dependent refer to actors in the general relation of dependence (and, of course, also in the two models).

We have just outlined the importance of the candidate's demand for protection and his acceptance. In the feudal model, this initial agreement is formalised and public. Help is sought in a stock formula and received in the same way. A rite, simple or ceremonious, with prescribed words and gestures indicates that henceforth the two men are lord and vassal. The ceremony makes the feudal tie public. A certain individual is known to have become the vassal of a certain lord. In contrast, the initial agreement between two persons entering into a relation of clientship is neither formalised nor public; it may even be tacit.

The rights and obligations of vassal and lord are specified in the written or oral 'charter of the institution'. This charter (in the Malinowskian sense of the term), pre-exists the feudal relations which are being created, and cannot be changed by the parties, just as when a man and woman marry, they cannot change the matrimonial roles as they are defined by their society. In what we are here calling clientship, client and patron are, to a large extent, free to determine the content of their respective roles. They are guided by various usages according to the type of clientship. Thus in our industrial societies, the clients of a politician, a great surgeon, a show-business celebrity, or an influential businessman expect different kinds of protection from their patrons, and offer them very different kinds of service.

The feudal charter also provides for sanctions if one of the parties does not fulfil his obligations. The vassal who considers himself injured, the lord who thinks he has been cheated, have some redress. Regular tribunals or special courts of arbitration deal with feudal matters. Under certain conditions, moreover (indemnity, for example), the relationship can end just as it has begun – of the parties' own accord. In the clientship relation, on the other hand, the only sanction is rupture, and the courts do not regard the relationship of dependence as having legal significance.

The two models really express an identical relationship – that of dependence/protection. In the final analysis, their only difference lies in the fact that feudal dependence is institutionalised while the dependence of clientship is not. The first, like marriage, is a societal relation which gives rise to a network called by a name known to all members of the society. The second, like a liaison, is an interpersonal relationship, fluid in content, without legal consequences. It is essentially a private affair and socially almost invisible.

Rwandan origins of the model

Clientship, patron and client are terms which obviously evoke the plebeian of ancient Rome who put himself under the protection of a patrician and became his client. Feudality, lord and vassal naturally refer us to a central institution of the Middle Ages in Europe. Why use notions so completely alien to the African heritage to describe and analyse social phenomena in traditional Africa?

The best way of answering this question seems to be to trace the development of the research which led us to use the feudal model. Here is what actually happened.

The author, in the 1950s, carried out anthropological research in Rwanda. It was concerned with the social relations of the traditional period, and in particular the last years of this period, 1890–1910. It dealt with a relatively recent past (there were many witnesses of the period still living), and one of which important fragments still functioned (for them, one could proceed by direct observation). A body of relations known as *ubuhake* seemed to be particularly important to the Rwandans. It had already been noticed by scholars interested in the ancient culture of the kingdom.

Having studied *ubuhake* by the usual field methods, the anthropologist gave a description of them which can be summarised as follows. In *ubuhake* (the noun comes from a verb meaning 'to pay a visit of homage') one man promised another to make him certain prestations of goods or services, and begged him for the use of one or more head of cattle. If the offer (expressed according to a customary formula) was accepted, the man making the request became the *garagu* and the man giving the cattle the *shebuja*.

Shebuja and *garagu* corresponded to two roles, the reciprocal rights and duties of which were well known to everyone in Rwandan society. The *garagu* was entitled to the usufruct of the cattle he had been given (milk, young bulls), while the ownership remained with the *shebuja*; the *garagu* could, moreover, in a general way obtain his *shebuja*'s support through all life's difficulties. In return he would render to his *shebuja* any services asked of him; these would vary with the status of the *garagu*.

The *shebuja* who entrusted cattle to his *garagu* was a Tutsi (except in some rare and exceptional cases). The *garagu* was either a Tutsi (whose obligations were then those of counsellor, messenger or courtier) or a Hutu (who would regularly present his *shebuja* with some produce from his fields and would work for him part of the time). Whether Tutsi or Hutu, the *garagu* benefited from the protection of the *shebuja*; this was culturally expected, even if the extent of the protection was left to the discretion of the *shebuja*.

The *ubuhake* tie could be ended at any time if one of the parties so desired. But it would obviously be unwise for a Hutu *garagu* to exercise this right against the wishes of his Tutsi *shebuja* without previously gaining the support of another Tutsi, who would thus become his new *shebuja*. On the death of one of the parties, the tie was usually maintained by his heir, but there was no renewal by tacit agreement. Both demand and acceptance had to be renewed[1].

The anthropologist, in describing all this, has taken care to leave key-words referring to the relationship and the two actors in the language of Rwanda. The *ubuhake* network was distinguished from other relations by the Rwandans themselves, because they called them by specific names. The author might, obviously, have been content to give an ethnographic description. But anthropology goes further; like any proper cognitive discipline, it compares and explains. Description showed that *ubuhake* was an original network which did not fit into the usual categories of kinship, marriage,

The sacred drum of the Rwanda monarchy. This large drum, called Kalinga, **199** was never beaten; it was identified with kingly power. The smaller one was beaten in its honour. The granular appearance of Kalinga is due to the blood of sacrificed animals which is periodically smeared on it; the circular objects on top of it contain the genitals of slain enemy chiefs.

government and stratification. Was it unique? To what could it be compared? To answer those questions, one had to look at relations and situations showing similarities to *ubuhake* in other societies.

First the author considered the neighbouring societies to Rwanda in the cultural area of the Great Lakes. These societies, which have so much in common owing to the small number of the points of origin of their population, to several centuries of common history, and to the use of the same productive techniques in a similar environment, were they endowed with institutions similar to the *ubuhake*? In perusing the anthropological record of these societies, one could discover three institutions similar to *ubuhake*. They existed in Ankole, Burundi, and the chiefdoms of Buha. We have not found any trace of equivalent networks elsewhere.

Here is a short description of the three institutions. Among the Nkole, the term *toisha* applied to a man who had sworn to the king (*gabe*) that he would follow him to war, and who had promised to give him a certain number of cattle from time to time. The king protected his *toisha* against raids on his cattle, or helped him to recover them if they were stolen. When a *toisha* did lose a herd, the king would give him a few other cattle to start a new one. Finally when two *toisha* quarrelled, the king acted as arbitrator. Only warrior-herdsman members of the Hima caste could become *toisha* of the king. Thus the *okutoisha* relationship existed only within the Hima caste. The role of protector was the exclusive prerogative of the king. If any Hima other than the king were to accept warriors as *toisha*, he would be setting himself up as the king's rival. The king had then either to fight him or give in and cede the monarchy to him. The tie was a personal one. When a *toisha* died his successor had to re-establish the tie by giving the king what was known as a burial cow. A *toisha* could unilaterally put an end to the relationship by ceasing to fulfil the obligations of his role[2].

In Burundi, a man who wished to enter into a relation of *ubugabire* with someone more powerful would humbly court him, visiting him frequently with small presents. If, after a waiting period which could last several months, a cow (*ingabire*) was granted to the applicant, this marked the beginning of a new relationship between the two men, who would henceforth assume the roles of *gabire* and *shebuja*. The *gabire* worked for his *shebuja*, gave him pots of beer, and after the cow had calved several times, would give him a heifer. The handing over of a heifer would be repeated even after the disappearance of the original cow. If the *gabire* neglected his duties, the *shebuja* could take back the cow, and thus put an end to the tie which bound them. The *gabire*, in return for his prestations, obtained the protection of his *shebuja*. The institution of *ubugabire* could unite equals as well as superiors/inferiors. A *shebuja* could even be of lower status than his *gabire*. When two Tutsi formed an *ubugabire* relationship it was a matter of friendship. The actors were sometimes called by the very significant terms of 'father' or 'Tutsi' (for the *shebuja*) and 'son' or 'Hutu' (for the *gabire*)[3].

In the half-dozen or so Ha chiefdoms, the *shebuja* and *gabire* were united by the same *ubugabire* relation. The relation was created by the gift of one or more beasts. 'As a general rule' says J.H.Scherer, 'only one beast was given; a second might follow later, but this was not required'. The *gabire* could do what he liked with the cattle he had been given, but he was obliged to render certain services from time to time (they were not well-defined), give his *shebuja* gifts, mainly of beer, and behave toward him as an eager, attentive courtier. It seems that originally only Tutsi had been *shebuja*. Traces of this persist in the use of the expression 'my Ha' for 'my *gabire*'. Later *ubugabire* spread within the Tutsi caste, where it formalised friendly relations. Finally, Hutu became *shebuja* of other Hutu, and even of Tutsi. Scherer emphasises that in Ha societies, *ubugabire* was associated with feelings of trust between the partners, who often became excellent friends. It could even happen that a Tutsi *shebuja*, on his death-bed, entrusted his wife to his *gabire* even though he was Hutu. When one party put an end to the *ubugabire* relation, the *gabire* had to return only the original cows, or their equivalent, but not their progeny[4].

Induction of the dependence/protection model

An examination of the ethnographic documentation of the Great Lakes cultural area showed the anthropologist that the *ubuhake* of Rwanda was not unique. The obvious similarity between *ubuhake* and the three other institutions allowed him to abstract an original model of societal relation. The actors are in pairs (*shebuja/garagu*, *gabe/toisha*, *shebuja/gabire*), and the obligation of the one to protect, and of the other to render various services, is common to all their culturally defined roles. They also have in common the mutual choice of the actors, the formalised public commitment, the covenant, which is the origin of the relationship, and later justifies sanctions against shortcomings in the roles accepted. Thus, from a few concrete cases, we induced the elementary relation of dependence.

The anthropologist, realising that he had discovered America a few centuries after Christopher Columbus, was well aware that Africans of the Great Lake region were not the only ones who institutionalised relations of dependence. He remembered ancient Rome, traditional Japan and the Middle Ages in Europe, which had indeed already often been mentioned in connexion with the inter-lacustrine kingdoms. But in fact it was a general analogy between global societies that had been stressed. Thus, Buganda was found to be a feudal society because there was a king and a court, princes and nobles, warriors and peasants, court etiquette and obligatory labour (all characteristics which are not feudal by our definition). The Tutsi's haughty manner and aristocratic bearing contributed much to the feudal image of Rwanda. Be that as it may, the author's attention was turned to European feudality.

Medieval feudality, for historians, was a condition of the societies of Europe which lasted several centuries, although it obviously had been changing throughout this period. More precisely, it lasted from the middle of the ninth century to the beginning of the thirteenth in the states that were born of the break-up of the Carolingian empire. During that long period and over that wide geographical area there grew up a complex civilisation with different and changing social institutions. Among these, one can isolate an institution of dependence and protection, and abstract from it the same model as the one we induced from certain African institutions: namely, the feudal relation between lord and vassal. Originating in the homage ritual, on which the two actors fully commit themselves, the feudal covenant guarantees, according to the charter of the institution, protection for the vassal and military and economic prestations for the lord.

This institution was considered so important in the civilisation which dominated the greater part of Europe for three and a half centuries, that it gave its name to it. Consequently, when one speaks of a *feudal society* or *régime*, one is alluding to something much more all-embracing than the institution itself. It includes, for example, an extreme fragmentation of ownership rights, a hierarchy of land rights originating from this division[5], the peasant's servitude, and the domination of a specialised warrior class[6].

The anthropologist's attempt at comparison dealt only with the feudal institution and not the régime. The comparison was not applied either – it is important to make this clear – to feudality in the sense of a mode of production. In the Marxist analysis, feudality is seen as one of the three pre-capitalist modes of production. The basis of the relations of production in feudal society are the lord's ownership of the land and the limited rights of the producer, the peasant-serf. It was on the labour of the serfs that the feudal society was based[7]. In this interpretation of feudality, the tie of vassalage has disappeared – the only thing that is taken into account is the serf/landowner relationship, which also existed in medieval society but which is very different from feudality (among these differences is the fact that the serf/owner relationship was not voluntary).

The anthropologist therefore isolated the feudal *institution*. The latter certainly has important aspects other than the tie of dependence. Thus, Fustel de Coulanges saw in it above all the fief of land that a lord gave to his vassal, which constituted a particular kind of possession of real property. There is, moreover, an interesting parallel between the fief and the cattle that a protector in Africa gives to his dependent. In both systems we are concerned with goods of which the dependent receives possession but not ownership, and which are granted to him as proof of the acceptance of his services, and as a way of enabling him to make prestations. Be that as it may, for most European experts on the Middle Ages, such as Bloch, Ganshof and Stephenson, the crucial factor is not the fief, but the vassal tie, the relation between lord and vassal[8].

In calling the model of institutionalised dependence relations 'feudal', the author wished to emphasise the comparative significance of a relation abstracted from a few African cases, by referring to a well-known historical institution. In the social sciences, it is rare to coin a new word (*anomie*, for example), but one designates phenomena, especially institutions, by terms which were applied originally to particular historical periods (thus *royalty* is derived from Roman history, *clan* from Scottish and Irish history, and *politics* from the cities of ancient Greece).

Retainers have always and everywhere gathered around an

important man, expecting much of him, tying their fortune to his, serving him. It is important to distinguish this kind of dependency, which is universal, from institutionalised dependency, which is not (the first is probably rooted in man's social nature and the second in cultural diversity). The term clientship, which also originates in historical situations (pre-Imperial Rome, the monarchy of the Franks in the Merovingian period), has acquired in our language a meaning which comes close to 'fluid dependence'. That is why the author thought it useful to use the term for the more flexible tie of protection as opposed to the feudal pact[9].

These were the stages of the journey undertaken by the author, starting with field-work in Rwanda, and ending with the formal model of feudality. Having demonstrated that African institutions can be validly compared with others of feudal type, we return to matters we had temporarily put aside.

Functions of traditional feudalities

In Ankole, the feudal relation was formed exclusively in the superior caste of Hima, and if each tie was a voluntary one, there could still only be one lord for all the Hima, who was also the king, they say, because he was known as *gabe*. This combination of feudal role (lord) and political role (king) in a single person, and the possibility of a challenge (if another Hima began to recruit vassals, the king would have to fight him) shows that in Ankole, for members of the superior caste, the feudal institution replaced the political network. They chose from their own ranks a protector to whom they paid homage. But this common lord was not really a king for the Hima, because they were not subject to coercion. If some Hima broke the feudal covenant, as custom allowed them to do, and transferred their allegiance to someone else, the balance of power was disturbed, and the king-lord had to try to re-establish it in his favour, by various means, which might possibly include armed combat, fighting between factions, but not police intervention. The genealogies of the hereditary kings mask this reality, which the institutions reveal. In Ankole, the superior caste practised the kind of feudality which Coulborn calls 'a method of government in which the essential relation is not that between ruler and subject, nor state and citizen, but between lord and vassal'[10]. We should say rather that the feudal institution took the place of a political network which did not exist among the Hima, and fulfilled for them the function of directing public affairs. In the other Great Lakes societies the feudal network did not fulfil this function. There, it had been assumed by a governmental network. However, for the Iru peasants, the common lord of the Hima was indeed king, since he was in a position to use coercion against them.

As lord and vassal were both necessarily Hima, the Nkole feudal network fulfilled the second function of strengthening the solidarity of the superior caste. The kin groups of herdsmen scattered among the cultivators might have diluted their aristocratic blood. *Okutoisha*, by its exclusive nature, maintained their sense of identity. It also contributed to the solidarity of the Hima stratum by organising within it a continual redistribution of cattle, which was certainly not intended to produce economic equality, but which guaranteed all Hima the use of the cattle without which they could not lead the life of a pastoral aristocracy. A kind of collective insurance against the loss of cattle, the mechanism of protection was a safeguard for individuals against loss of social status.

This function of the solidarity within one stratum was also very clearly shown in Rwanda by the *ubuhake* tie between Tutsi. It was less evident, it seems, in Burundi and Buha, where more emphasis was placed on friendship than on a militant display of caste solidarity.

Table 2

Networks of inequality		Feudal networks	
Superior/inferior relation		Institution	Lord/vassal relation
Ankole	Hima/Iru	*okutoisha*	*gabe/toisha*
Rwanda	Tutsi/Hutu/Twa	*ubuhake*	*shebuja/garagu*
Burundi	Tutsi/Hima/ Hutu/Twa	*ubugabire*	*shebuja/gabire*
Ha Chiefdoms	Tutsi/Ha	*ubugabire*	*shebuja/gabire*

The third function of the feudal network was to turn superior status to material advantage. We have already pointed out above that aristocratic status facilitated the exercise of undue pressure, but that in itself it did not give a right to goods or services. In Ankole, where the system seems to have been very rudimentary, the use of pressure was still a matter for individuals. In Rwanda, it was possible for a peasant to protect himself against unexpected but predictable Tutsi pressure by becoming a dependent of one Tutsi. *Ubuhake* was above all a relationship between a Tutsi lord and a Hutu vassal. The latter paid tribute to his *shebuja* in produce from his fields and in manual labour. When the extortionate aspect of *ubuhake* was denounced at the end of the colonial period, the Tutsi claimed that the goods and services provided by their dependent peasants were no more than a return for the material benefits accruing from the cattle the Tutsi lords had given them. We do not think this was so. Usually the peasant received no more than one or two beasts. The usufruct consisted mainly of milk, which was not available for human consumption until the calf had had its share, and of the bull-calves that the cow produced. It was largely for the Tutsi lord himself to decide how much was due to him in prestations of goods and labour. In these circumstances, one cannot agree that this was an economic exchange.

In Rwanda, the feudal network supported the power relations which made the superior caste into the dominant one. This function, which was very advantageous for all the Tutsi, was particularly so for those who, not being rulers, had no share in the revenue from taxes and dues. The acquisition of consumer goods without working for them was institutionalised. In Burundi and Buha, the *ubugabire* network fulfilled the same function, but to a lesser degree; the obligations of the protected individual were lighter and less well defined.

A fourth function of these traditional feudal systems, the reverse of the previous one, was to make inequality bearable for the inferiors. Even if they had to pay for protection, they obtained it; other Tutsi than their lord left them in peace. And even if their prestations depended rather arbitrarily on their lord's goodwill, there were acknowledged norms, and when these were flagrantly ignored the peasant vassal could discreetly try to change his protector. Again, this function seemed less important in Burundi and Buha, where stratification was more vaguely defined, and less rigid than in Rwanda.

If men of unequal status maintain continuing individual relations, if they are on the same side in certain disputes, or if peasants can make use of even a precarious right to some cattle, the pastoral value *par excellence* – all these links, perpendicular to the division of the global society into horizontal strata, helped to lessen conflict within the society. This fifth function, obviously absent in Ankole and clearly present in Rwanda and Burundi, was carried to its extreme in Buha, where the feudal relation could be the

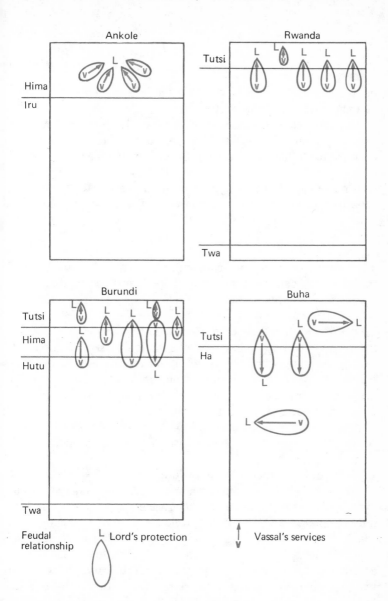

Figure 8   Stratification and feudality: four variants

opposite of the inequality relation: the lord could be of inferior and the vassal of superior status.

We come finally to the last function: friendly mutual aid between two individuals. The institutionalised form of protection/dependence seems to have been used in Burundi by two men who wished to give formal recognition, and no doubt legal consequences, to their pact of solidarity, and, perhaps, to their peculiar affection too (sexual ambivalence was not unknown to Tutsi aristocrats).

Some hypotheses

This somewhat academic enumeration of the six functions of traditional feudalities in the Great Lakes is justified by the insight it gives into the feudal network itself, and by the perspectives it offers for a comparative study.

Of these six functions only one, the last – the solemnisation of friendship – is independent of any situation of stratification. All the others can operate only where there exists a network of inequality. Is the feudal institution only incidental to a network of inequality? Or does one normally find a feudal network in societies with a superior caste? Our first conclusion from this examination of functions leads us to advance a hypothesis to be verified by later comparative research: the feudal institution shows a high correlation with stratification.

What does it do there? It has a two-fold effect. First, the network of allegiance it creates among superiors, plus the material advantages it assures them, maintains heterogeneity. Secondly, it lessens internal conflict by moderating exploitation and by creating ties which cut across the lines separating castes. These two actions have the total effect of balancing the inequality system, thus assuring its continuity. We can translate this interpretation into two hypotheses: the feudal network re-inforces the superior caste;

it also acts as a buffer in the struggle between castes.

In this study of power, we are particularly interested in another function: turning superiority to material advantage. Aristocratic status would have no power without the prestations of goods and services which go up, as it were, from the inferiors to the superiors through the feudal network. Inequality artificially creates the need for protection of inferiors. Feudality organises the purchase of that protection. By this mechanism, the superior, if he was a lord, obtained goods and services without an equivalent return. This is power. We will now advance the following hypothesis: the feudal network translates status into power.

The function of feudality as a substitute for a political system which was observed in Ankole, draws our attention to something else. In a group of equals such as the Hima warrior-herdsmen, who are not disposed to accept the exercise of constraint by one man on the rest, individual dependence makes it possible to entrust all leadership to a common lord. One obeys him because one has entered into a pact with him. The lord does not rule, he protects his vassals who, having put their trust in him, follow him. But they are not subjects. If they consider that the lord does not adequately perform his task, they withdraw their trust. They are always entitled to do so (the feudal choice is revocable) and they often have the possibility (if they have been alert enough to prevent the lord from developing an apparatus of constraint like a king's). This interpretation of facts in Ankole, which seems to be confirmed by some situations in medieval Europe, leads to the following hypothesis: in a group of equals, the feudal institution can replace the political network.

Like the blood pact in other societies, the rite of the feudal contract in Buha makes public and finally binding a bond of friendship which is more commonly a private affair. The final hypothesis is as follows: the feudal covenant transforms a fluid relation of friendship, one without obligations, into a relationship with form and content fixed by a charter.

The six functions identified in the traditional feudalities of the Great Lakes could not co-exist in the same society. They are not all compatible. The same is true of the hypotheses just advanced. They could not all be verified from the feudal network of a given society; but perhaps they can all be in the same feudal institution. This seems to confirm the validity of an analytical approach which starts from formal, non-functional models.

Synchronic and diachronic aspects of feudality

It is possible to follow kinship, marriage, government and in-equality networks right through the traditional, colonial and independent periods of Black Africa. One cannot do this with the feudal institution. Traditional feudal institutions no doubt survived the colonial conquest, but the new conditions weakened them. The progressive disappearance of the old aristocracies made a lord's protection superfluous and feudal prestations fell into disuse in a monetary economy.

New feudal networks were not formed. The institutionalisation of ties of dependence between individuals is incompatible with modern collective representations. In both colonial and independent Africa, of course, powerful or eminent men attracted, and still attract, loyalty, devotion and hopes. They became, and become, the patrons of zealous clients. In colonial societies with clear-cut stratification, the immemorial need for the protection of inferiors was always present. Being 'the black of a certain white' could help one avoid trouble such as being picked for compulsory labour, fined for some minor offence, or refused credit in a shop. In the independent states, ministers and important officials are surrounded by clients. The relation of individual dependence is usually based on another relation: kinship, affinity, or common tribal origin.

These relations of clientship, important as they are, are not strictly our concern. They are difficult to discern, as they are confidential and partly clandestine, and being interpersonal and culturally indeterminate, they cannot constitute a societal network.

As the feudal networks we have considered had no successors, it seems that we cannot hope to understand their evolution. The descriptions of *okutoisha*, *ubuhake* and *ubugabire* on which our analysis is based are indeed synchronic. They relate to the period 1890–1910. Fortunately, as we saw in the preceding chapter, we are not altogether ignorant of the past of Ankole, Rwanda, Burundi, and Buha. From all that we know about their history, we can try to put the institutions observed at the end of the nineteenth century into an historical perspective. That is to say, try to translate the synchronic varieties of the feudal model into the diachronic stages of an evolutionary sequence.

Ankole, at least the northern part (according to the boundaries established in the nineteenth century) is situated in the territory which was, from the thirteenth to fifteenth century, the kingdom of Kitara. In the fifteenth century, the ruling dynasty of Kitara was that of the Chwezi. According to Nkole traditions (perhaps ancient, though we know only recent versions) the Chwezi were herdsmen who created a brilliant civilisation. The king and a numerous court lived in huge huts surrounded by large enclosures; artisans made bark-cloth, practised the art of digging wells through rock, and constructed fortifications. As we mentioned earlier, towards the end of the fifteenth century, Nilotic Luo herdsmen invaded Kitara and founded in its place Bunyoro, ruled by the Bito dynasty. The part of Kitara which was to become Ankole was not invaded by the Bito, but by another clan, the Hinda, who are Hima related to the Chwezi. This historical event – the conquest of part of the old kingdom of Kitara by a group of Hima – is disguised in Nkole traditions in stories of marvels (the Chwezi are said to have been swallowed up by Lake Victoria), and falsified so that the myth of dynastic continuity can be respected (the story goes that Ruhinda, son of the last Chwezi king Wamara, allowed a peasant to persuade him not to go into the lake; abandoning all the other Chwezi, he came back with a drum, the symbol of monarchy, and founded Ankole[11]).

The Nkole variant of the feudal institution, *okutoisha*, was perfectly adapted to the conquest situation. The Hinda, who were small bands of warriors and herdsmen, needed to strengthen their cohesion in opposition to the Iru peasants. Their recent nomadic style of life, too, had not prepared them to accept a network of constraint. *Okutoisha* met their needs very well.

From the sixteenth to the nineteenth centuries, the Tutsi of Rwanda were engaged in the slow process of subjugating the small isolated peasant communities which were scattered throughout their pastoral domains. Their need was to stabilise the conquest into stratification, and then to ensure its efficacy and endurance. *Ubuhake*, the Rwanda variant of the feudal institution, is a remarkable instrument which balances exploitation and protection, solidarity of superiors and cohesion of all. It corresponds to this stage of evolution.

It is probable that the Hinda clan also was at the origin of Burundi. But we know less about the history of this kingdom, which in the nineteenth century was as large as Rwanda. The centralisation and despotism so strongly stressed by the Rwanda king Rwabugiri at the end of his reign – which lasted from 1860/5 till 1895 – have no parallel in Burundi. There, at the end of the traditional period, centres of influence and wealth were more numerous: important lineages, princely families, high nobility. This more fluid situation softened the rigour of the feudal institu-

Table 3 Three variants of the feudal model

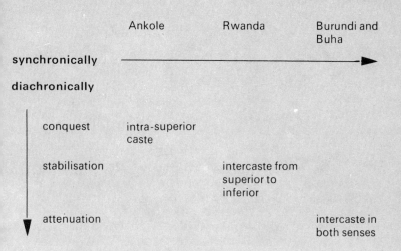

	Ankole	Rwanda	Burundi and Buha
synchronically →			
diachronically ↓			
conquest	intra-superior caste		
stabilisation		intercaste from superior to inferior	
attenuation			intercaste in both senses

tion of *ubugabire* and gave it a new function, mutual aid on an exclusively individual basis. This function, which remained secondary in Burundi, assumed great importance in the Buha chiefdoms, which were probably founded in the eighteenth century by Tutsi emigrants from Burundi, who established a sort of marginal and simplified Rundi society.

This attempt to put synchronic variants of the same institutional model into diachronic perspective is, of course, highly hypothetical. It aims less at reconstructing an historic sequence than at emphasising the coherence between three social stages (conquest, stabilisation of inequality, mitigation of stratification), and three forms of feudality (limited to the superior caste, predominantly intercaste, and oriented towards mutual aid). It is no more than a possibility that these three feudal forms actually succeeded each other in that order.

Networks of dependence/protection institutionalised in feudalities were not very widespread in traditional Africa. It seems that they only developed out of caste stratification, which immediately rules out a great many societies. On the other hand, as feudality is not as common an anthropological category as kinship, marriage, government, etc., very little research has been directed to the phenomena of dependence. The four societies whose feudal institutions we have just analysed are certainly not the only ones to possess any. In West Africa, the feudal organisation of the Bariba of Dahomey has been given great attention by Jacques Lombard[12]. Unfortunately, such works are too rare for a comparative analysis of the whole of Sub-Saharan Africa to be possible.

9 Association

It is night in a village in Yoruba country, and a group of men are marching in procession. Their faces are hidden by masks, and their bodies disappear under ample garments of woven grass. Some of them rapidly twirl a rhombus which emits a disturbing sound, a sort of savage roaring. The silent villagers take shelter in their homes. They know that the *Oro* brotherhood are holding a ceremony, and that to be caught even looking at them is to risk death. They know, too, that tonight the brotherhood is going to seize upon some condemned person and put him to death. Among the Sara, in the Chadian savanna, men dressed in lion-skins, wearing wooden soles which leave marks like a lion's tracks and armed with iron claws, lie in ambush, waiting for a man to come along whom they will seize and sell as a slave. Among the Hamba in the Congolese Equatorial forest, in the village square, the 'masters of the forest' are ceremonially seated in a circle around a pangolin, which only members of the association are entitled to consume. Among the Bambara of the Upper Niger region, every man has to become a member of six societies in succession in the course of his lifetime, if he wants to acquire progressively all the esoteric knowledge of the world and of myths, and if he wants to share in the vital forces from which men and the gods take their origin. Entry into each of these six societies – *Ntomo*, *Komo*, *Nama*, *Kono*, *Tyiwara* and *Kore* – was marked by an initiation[1].

These few pictures of the traditional past – though the term used is the 'ethnographic present' – make one appreciate the complexity of African associations. Whether they are secret or public, useful or criminal, supported by terror or prestige, or pursuing different ends linked to religious or magical systems of representation, these associations all share in common the fact that they are 'fraternities', established by a conjunction of purposeful intentions with a view to achieving specific ends.

Left Among the Lega (Eastern Congo-Kinshasa), men of wealth belong to the Bwame association. Here they are performing the pangolin ritual dance. (A pangolin is a scaly ant-eater.)
This page In the criminal association of the lion-men of Saraland in Chad, members wore wooden soles imitating lions' footprints, and killed their victims with the forged iron weapon resembling lion's claws.

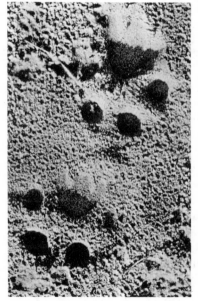

The relation of voluntary fraternity

From this wealth of aspects and cultural traits associated with African associations – masks and dances, beliefs and myths, public ceremonies and furtive practices, philosophical wisdom and brutality of action – we shall consider only the sociological reality: association as a network of relations.

Associations, from this point of view, are societies, 'permanent groups of people with organised activities'. Up to now, we have only come across one type of society, the global society. An association is far less all-embracing. Whereas the global society co-ordinates all the activities of its members in such a way that they can live together from birth to death, and that the group is perpetuated over several generations, an association gathers together those who pursue in common certain limited objectives.

An association, *vis-à-vis* other societal relations, presents a particular kind of ambiguity. Like other relations, it is first a relationship between associates who agree to conform to rules which they themselves, or their predecessors, have established. In the event of a breach of these rules, they agree to submit to sanctions, often very severe, which are meted out to the transgressor by his associates. But in addition, and this is the new feature, the society's most efficacious action is most often directed against non-members. Individuals who are not voluntarily committed to any network of relations find themselves engaged, usually against their will, in relations with the associates. As these relations are the result of an agreement between associates, let us first consider what we can call the *internal* relation of association.

In traditional Africa, new associations were not readily formed. Innovation, in this as well as other areas, was more suspect than sought. The founders of a society preferred to have some link with past events or persons, or even to borrow from their neighbours.

The bond of fraternity of the members
of the hornbill association among the
Nyanga in Congo-Kinshasa. Here their
dancing forms part of the initiation
rites of the young boys of the tribe.

Thus 'the *Simo* spread all over Lower Guinea among the Susu, Baga and Nalu; the *Poro* in Upper Guinea and Sierra Leone, among the Mende, Temne, Guerze, Toma and others'[2]. In most cases, from an individual's point of view, the association pre-existed his desire to enter it and, for him, it was only a question of being admitted. This admission depended on passing certain tests, the payment of entrance fees, and on the acceptance of the new member by the 'brothers'.

The tests to be undergone recall the institution of initiation which is so widespread in Black Africa. African initiation developed in another context – the course of individual life whose essential dividing point, puberty, separating childhood from adolescence, it so clearly and forcefully marks. Besides the passing of tests which show that the boy or girl concerned possess the necessary courage, endurance and skills to perform their adult roles, initiation had an educational content and a ritual aspect.

The ceremony properly speaking – which is a passage ritual

Sometimes a voluntary association
is based on a common initiation. Bead
masks are worn after the initiation
by Sara girls in Chad.

223

loaded with symbols of death to the old life and re-birth in the
new – is preceded by a period of probation which may last several
months, in which the initiates' instructor or instructress teaches
them the conduct expected of adults and the reasons for it. The
rite of entrance to an association retained at least the test part of
initiation. The candidate had to perform a dangerous and often
difficult mission in order to prove that he was capable of partici-
pating in the activities of the group. In the secret societies of
sorcerers and criminals, the test could be murder.

In associations of men of standing such as that of the 'masters of
the forest', what mattered was to display one's wealth by handing
over valuable goods to the association, and by giving a huge feast.
Finally, after a trial period, the associates would either admit the
candidate or refuse him entrance. If he was accepted, he would
become an actor in an internal relation of association.

Like marriage alliance and feudality, it is at the same time a
relation in principle voluntary and one with roles determined by a
charter, that of the association. But two new elements enter into it:
first, one of the actors is a 'moral person', and secondly, association
roles are not necessarily recognised by the total society.

In the case we are considering here, the most common one,
which is the admission of a new member (and not the foundation
of a new society), a tie is established between the new associate and
the association as such, and not between a recent associate and
each of the older members. Borrowing a Western legal concept, we
can say that an association is a 'moral being', that is to say that it
can act like a physical person; it can accept or refuse a candidate
and it has various rights and obligations towards him. It makes its
will known through the intermediacy of men, its members, according to the norms that are characteristic of a given association, and
are part of its oral 'charter'. This concept of 'moral being' is introduced here as a tool in the anthropologist's outfit. We do not

affirm, we do not think that the concept of moral personality actually existed in the idea systems of traditional Africa (in the same way that it is part of our explicit legal theories), but we think it is useful in accounting for observed facts. It is the same with the term 'charter'.

As associations are not the first groupings we have encountered – we have spoken of lineages and clans, tribes and states – it might seem strange that this concept of corporate body was not adopted before. Until now, indeed, the relations between roles ascribed to physical beings have been sufficient for the analysis of societal networks. Has the notion of corporate body not been developed in our own legal doctrine specifically to apply to associations? Associations pose many other new kinds of problem.

One of these problems is the recognition granted by the global society to these association roles. Some members of a society form an association with the aim of pursuing ends of their own. Why would others institutionalise what is organised apart from them, or even against them?

Let us take the extreme case of an association of criminals. Note that this case is rare. If we have given the impression that among African associations there are many fraternities of sorcerers – a feeling one often gets from reading anthropological works – it is because we know relatively more about this kind of association than about most others, thanks to the archives of the colonial tribunals. The trials of the *aniota*, the Congo leopard-men, the Chad lion-men, and of the Azande secret societies accused of cannibalism, led to the accumulation of reports of enquiries and prosecution documents. But one category of facts is unrepresented among those which gave rise to legal action. A sorcerer, in traditional Africa, was an individual who did evil, chiefly by using magic. Considered as a criminal, he risked his life if he was discovered. But inasmuch as he was suspected of evil powers, he was feared. An association of sorcerers presented an even more serious threat to a village or region. Political authorities condemned them, and fought against them. To them, these were *de facto* associations to which they did not grant any recognition.

Most of the 'brotherhoods' had purposes which were either of no consequence to non-members, or in principle useful to the collectivity. In the first category were the churches where the initiates of a certain cult met to worship their god. In the second, there were societies which exercised judicial or religious functions for the whole community, or others which expressed and magnified the social reprobation incurred by people who behaved in an unpopular way without committing an offence punishable by the chief (for example, evasion of collective labour, habitual quarrelling, failure to pay debts). Thus for example men of the *molimo* association of the Ituri forest pygmies made a noise outside the hut of anyone who had endangered the solidarity of the·band by refusing to settle a quarrel[3].

Associates and out-groups

Relations between associates form the interior network of the fraternity, and associates have roles among themselves which are prescribed by the charter of their society. These relations are fundamental, since they give rise to the roles of associate, out of which is woven the *societal* network between associates, on the one hand, and on the other the members of the global society who do not belong to the association, the out-groups. The elementary relation which generates this network – let us call it the association's *external* relation – comprises two actors: the associate and the out-group, and their roles are defined in relationship to the ends and the strength of the association.

Among the Ibibio in Nigeria, when a member of the *Ekpo*

society was in contact with a non-member, their respective roles were determined by the aim of the association (the maintenance of order in the name of the ancestors) and by the considerable pressure that this association was able to apply to all Ibibio who did not adhere to it. The relationship between a group member and a non-member is always asymmetrical (since one obviously cannot reverse the relations between the actors) and is always an expression of tension between two unequal forces (the group member being supported by his associates, whereas the non-member is isolated).

An association is essentially a group of men inside a global society, who combine to apply pressure on others in order to attain their common goal. Political supremacy, an important position in the kinship network, or superiority of status, carry weight; the union of the associates, also. Once the pressure group is formed, the weight it can apply becomes more important than the aim itself. A cult-association, for example, can warp its objective and use its force to promote masculine domination over women.

It is understandable, from this point of view, that rulers have generally been a little uneasy about associations, all associations. They do constitute foci of pressure which are independent of the political power, and thus potentially dangerous to it. In the West African monarchies, however, where there were numerous associations performing tasks more commonly reserved for rulers, conflicts seem to have been rare. They were certainly minimised by the combination of important governmental and association roles in the same individual. Elsewhere, among the Ibo for example, the division of responsibility was firmly established, and the association became a sort of governmental organ.

The ordinary members of global societies who did not belong to a fraternity had very little protection against its activities. Associations used various means to apply pressure. The sheer terrorism of the leopard-men was rather rare. Belief in the extravagant and evil powers of witchcraft aroused considerable fear which was utilised by some clandestine societies.

But the ability of the associations to persuade depended chiefly on religious beliefs. The wooden fibre and masks, which covered not only the wearer's face but his whole body, were hidden by the society in some secret place. Members usually wore them only for ceremonies, which were generally held at night. At this time, the mask and its human bearer became the incarnation of an ancestral spirit or a god. They were no longer simply a piece of carved wood and a man belonging to an association, but the indispensable support given to enable some immaterial being to be seen and heard. It would be an over-simplification to see this only as a fraud perpetrated by the association. Fellows of the fraternity could not reveal to an out-group (especially women and children) that they were behind the mask. Outsiders were supposed to believe that spirits had indeed emerged from the savanna or forest without human aid; association members certainly knew this to be untrue. But this is no reason to question their faith in temporary possession by spirits of the masks and themselves. Among Africans of the traditional period, the survival of ancestral spirits and the rather morose interest they took in their descendants were firmly established beliefs. By expressing the precise desires of the ancestors, the masked associates had a very efficacious means of action at their disposal.

In the associations of notables, where both entrance and promotion from one grade to the next were obtained by wealth, the means of pressure were prestige and fame. Members as they were of a very exclusive club, they combined the social prestige that each already had as an individual and so increased its weight. Societies which introduced members by degrees of esoteric knowledge wielded power over outsiders because the latter respected knowledge, which they thought gave power over the forces and energies of nature.

Associations in modern Africa

That the union and organisation of individuals are enough to produce a force which makes itself felt throughout the society where it appears is confirmed by what happened in the colonies. Freedom of association, whether or not it was legally guaranteed, was everywhere restricted. It was too dangerous for the colonial régime to allow Africans to form associations without some kind of control, even if these associations had no political objectives. When an association exists, it can use its power to achieve ends other than those included in its charter. In the Belgian Congo, the *Abako* was a harmless association of people of Kongo language and culture, who, living in Léopoldville (now Kinshasa), wanted to study and preserve the oral literature, dances and visual arts of the traditional Kongo. Shortly before independence *Abako* became an important movement in the anti-colonial struggle, and then a political party.

During the colonial period, certain religious associations given to the propagation of new cults incorporating both Christian and traditional elements, and certain trade-union type professional

Members of some voluntary associations, in order to apply pressure on out-groups, appear at night wearing masks intended to terrorise them. Women and children are particularly threatened and are thought to die if they once see the masks. *Left* Mask representing a baboon for the Kona association from the Dan tribal complex (Guinea). *Far left* Mask of the Babembe secret association from the Kube tribe (Congo-Kinshasa). *Below* A mask showing a beautiful girl, to be worn by an acrobatic dancer.

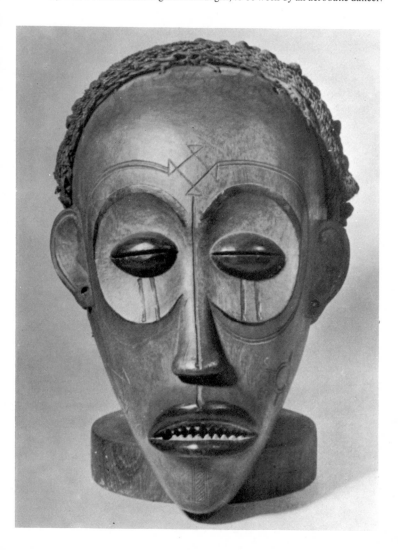

associations, were outlawed again and again by the rulers. The older associations of the preceding period were easily suspected of illegal practices, and were closely watched.

In independent Africa, the one-party presidential régimes and the military governments distrust associations just as much. Where there is only one authorised political party, associations which can call this exclusiveness in question obviously cannot be allowed. On the other hand, like certain brotherhoods of the traditional period, the single party is closely tied to the government (in the same way, by the combination of leading roles in a single person) and exercises some of the prerogatives of political authorities.

In modern as much as in traditional Africa, the societal network of association channels power relations. An association as such, as a corporate body, is a pressure group which is able by various means to inflict serious deprivation on outsiders, be they ordinary individuals (who can be deprived of life, health, the goodwill of the ancestors, or their possessions), or institutionalised groups (rulers, whose régimes can be challenged). This pressure which an association can exert confers on each of its members individually a certain amount of power. Each associate can to some extent (and this can be considerable if the man involved is an association leader) divert the pressure of the group from one outsider to another. To be spared this, the out-group seeks the protection of one or more associates. A familiar problem which we know can very simply be solved by a few gifts, goods or services. . . .

10 Exchange of goods

The economic network stems from the exchange-of-goods relation. This is enough to indicate its importance. From the point of view of this book, exchange is, further, the antithesis of the power relation. In the latter, the dominant individual obtains goods and services from the dominated *without* an economic return; that is to say, without being obliged to provide the latter with other commodities or prestations. In the exchange relation, an actor obtains goods and services from another actor, and *in return* provides other goods and services. These two relations are in perfect opposition to one another. What we shall say about the exchange relation will throw some light on the power relation.

In common usage, the term 'economic' is not limited to exchange. It includes the production, distribution and consumption of goods. From the anthropological viewpoint, production, it seems to us, depends on the environment of a global society and on its techniques, and thus is a matter for ecological and technological study. The societal aspects of production, as well as distribution and consumption, are part of an anthropological investigation which starts from elementary relational model of economic exchange.

The elementary model of economic exchange

Exchange and reciprocity, like dependence and power, rarely are completely absent from any human relation. One could try to find evidence of exchange wherever it is perceptible, and interpret the social universe from this point of view. But for us it is a question of specifying one form of exchange: economic reciprocity.

This is very simple: it can be defined as giving up goods or services in return for other goods or services. The roles are symmetrical; each actor must give agreed economic values to the other. It is not easy to find a term to designate the actors in this relation, for most of the words that might do apply more to com-

merce, which is certainly exchange, but of a professional kind (one lives by it) and specialised (one buys so as to sell). The most suitable word is perhaps 'dealer', which suggests the idea of a business transaction and of an agreement involving some sort of negotiation.

Although conceptually very clear, the economic exchange relation is not always easy to distinguish from other transactions involving goods in some traditional African contexts. This is a crucial question, since our analysis of power in Africa depends largely on the distinction between an economic return and a return of another order. Are not a subject who brings baskets of sorghum and beans to the king, and the king who guarantees him protection from foreign invasion, exchanging goods and services? Or when a peasant-vassal builds an enclosure for his lord's cattle, and the lord protects him from the exactions of other lords, are they not engaged in reciprocal economic prestations?

There are two procedures for recognising economic values. The first is suitable for cultures we know only from the outside. It is quick, and gives valid, if crude, results. One can consider as economic all material goods which directly meet the basic needs of life in the area studied (foodstuffs for everyday consumption, ordinary clothing) and the material means necessary to produce these things, (fields, animals, tools). Economic services are the actions necessary for the production of these goods (manual work, and, where the operation demands it, management and direction).

High relief carved in wood by a contemporary artist of Lubumbashi (Congo-Kinshasa). An everyday village scene: men carry a slaughtered goat to a woman who is pounding cassava. (In the author's collection.)

The second way of identifying the economic is more precise. It assumes that the anthropologist has acquired some 'inside' knowledge. He then knows, like any other member of the society he is studying, under what circumstances different types of goods and services normally figure in transactions. He knows, for example, that one *exchanges* cassava for hoes, but that one *gives* the skin of a bush-cat. His intimate knowledge of the society thus allows him to define the sphere of economic values.

This question settled, another one arises. A peasant brings his chief the surplus from his millet harvest; a few months later there is an unexpected scarcity, and the chief distributes the millet from his granaries to the villagers. Or again, a farmer gives part of the produce of his fields to his lord; the lord gives him a cow, whose milk he is entitled to consume. In both these cases, each side gives up economic goods, but we do not interpret this as an exchange. How can one judge the economic equivalence of these two prestations?

The relative value of two commodities can only be evaluated through the operation of a market. If it is usual to exchange a litre of milk for three pounds of beans, one can calculate the respective value of the vassal's agrarian prestations and the lord's pastoral ones. But one rarely finds together all the conditions necessary for a comparison with market value. Once more, familiarity with the culture allows one to do without it. The redistribution that the chief performs is not guaranteed, is occasional, and is not proportionate to what has been given; for members of the society its context is political, not economic. The dependent does not really want the dairy produce, but the lord's protection; this is understood among all the peasants and herdsmen of this society.

Economic networks in traditional Africa

In our urban and industrialised societies, all goods circulate; and nearly all goods circulate through economic networks. It was quite a different matter in traditional Africa. For one thing, many goods did not circulate at all; they were consumed by the unit that produced them, and never went through a market., This auto-consumption applied to foodstuffs all over Black Africa. It was exceptional to have regularly to obtain one's food by exchange. This only applied to the craftsmen in the cities who, as we know, were few in number until the end of the nineteenth century except in such regions as the Sudanese savanna, the Niger valley in particular, and some parts of the West coast. Even there, in many cases, the artisan's wives and children cultivated fields at the edge of the town. The same thing applied to the common clothing of bark-cloth, leather, or fibre. They were made by the people who used them.

This peasant habit of auto-consumption limited goods for circulation to the surplus. Now vast areas of sub-Saharan Africa were confined to a subsistence economy; each unit of production consumed all that it produced. This applied to the hunting and gathering bands (who employed the least efficient techniques of acquisition), but also to the cultivators of the Equatorial rain forests and of the Guinea coast who planted manioc, and other edible roots. Even in regions where there was a greater agrarian yield – the Sudanese savanna, the southern savanna, and the

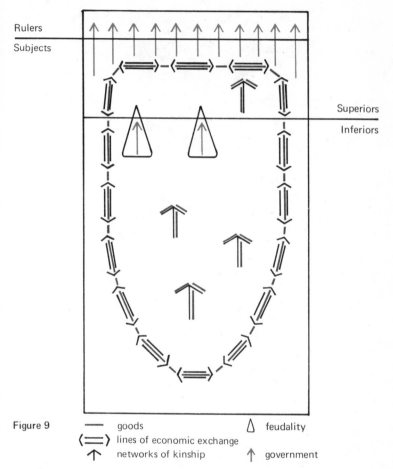

Rulers

Subjects

Superiors

Inferiors

Figure 9

— goods

(⚌) lines of economic exchange

↑ networks of kinship

△ feudality

↑ government

The different traditional channels of circulation of goods. In traditional societies, goods circulate not only along lines of economic exchange, but also through the networks of kinship, feudality and government.

Eastern high plateaux – there was never much of an agricultural surplus.

The goods which circulated were largely those which could not be produced locally: rare foodstuffs such as salt, iron weapons and tools, cotton and trade goods which, imported from Europe, were widespread over the whole continent before colonisation. There was a reverse flow in answer to this from the outside world. Black Africa exported luxury products: gold, ivory, skins, cola-nuts and woods for cabinet-making. And for four centuries, from the sixteenth to the nineteenth, it also exported men by the million (a serious calculation puts this demographic 'drain' at a total of fifteen to twenty million). These international exchanges were localised at certain points, those which were directly accessible by sea (East and West coast ports) and land (Sudanese towns where the trans-Saharan caravan routes ended). The rest of Africa was divided into many local and even familial autarkies. There was only a limited number of goods in circulation.

This circulation, moreover, only partly followed economic chan-

A market near Kisangani, Congo-Kinshasa. The   237
supply and demand economic model can be deduced
from the concrete transactions of the market place.

nels. The subject's role required him to pay taxes both in kind and
in labour work to chiefs and kings; the chiefs and kings, in turn,
maintained their officials, executive agents and courtiers, and
helped their subjects in times of need. This circulation of goods,
which has been called re-distribution, followed the political network. It did not go through a market[1]. The vassal's role obliged
him to make prestations of economic value, and the lord's role also
included some secondary prestations. Commodities circulated, then,
through the feudal network. A marriage alliance required the payment of bridewealth to the wife's kinship group, and after it had
been contracted, the husband benefited from his wife's work.
Inside the lineage, all the brothers joined in collective farm work.
Part at least of the international exchanges evaded the economic
network. Thus the circulation of gold at first followed a political
network (from subjects to monarch) and then an economic one
(from monarch to foreign traders).

According to the analysis we have just made, the circulation of
economic values through networks other than those of economic
exchange indicates a power relation. The chief, lord, king and
husband were using means of applying pressure that their roles gave
them access to in order to obtain goods.

There was also a market economy and markets. A market economy is synonymous with a network of economic exchanges. Our
dealer was not a purely rational *homo economicus*, seeking only
profit, whose behaviour was predictable enough for one to draw up
supply and demand curves. But he did act in an economic way:
wanting a certain good, he offered another so as to obtain it. His
'profit' lay less in a difference of value than in individual utility. He
obtained something he needed in return for something that was
less useful to him at that moment. Economic values were exchanged
everywhere. Certain places, at certain times, were used exclusively
for this purpose, and those were the markets.

Several prosperous African kingdoms had devised some sort
of monetary system long before the arrival of the Europeans.
A few societies of the southern savanna mined copper
and processed it. These copper crosses were used as a
medium of exchange. Each ingot is just over a foot long.

Markets and currencies

Markets of the traditional type – and some still exist – were very
pleasant places. There people met friends, exchanged news, heard
the latest domestic and political scandals, and intrigued for the
favours of important people or of a woman, all among the cheerful
buzz of conversation, vibrant colours in the bright sunshine, the
sweet cloying odours of the fruit, and the spicy perfume of
pimentos. People also enjoyed the safety which was explicitly
guaranteed by political authorities in the most important markets,
and which was customarily assured in all of them. Strictly economic
transactions only accounted for very small quantities of goods, in
the local markets since the parties to a deal had only a very small
surplus, their possibilities were very limited. But to prolong the
pleasure, they would haggle and bargain and try not to get rid of
their saleable merchandise too quickly[2].

In the regional and international markets, exchanges which were
naturally more important in terms of volume and value were
facilitated by the use of money, or rather by certain commodities
which more or less adequately fulfilled some of the functions of
money in modern economic systems. It is most unlikely that special
places for important transactions could have come into being
without some means of measuring the economic value of different
commodities, without an intermediary for exchanging them, and
without an instrument which could act as a store of value.

Metals are especially suitable for these different purposes. In
Sanga, in the province of Katanga in the present Congo-Kinshasa,
little copper crosses were found in the vast cemeteries which date
from the eighth century AD. These were used as money until the end
of the traditional period[3]. In the fourteenth century copper rods,
some thick and others thin, were used in the Nigerian savanna
kingdoms to pay for manual labour. Elsewhere, heavy rings called

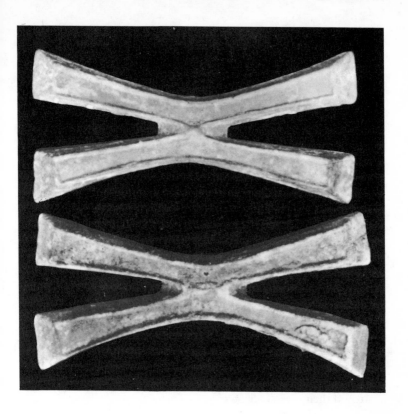

manillas served as a medium of exchange. Then there was gold. It was never made into coins, but in the Akan societies of the West African states gold dust, weighed on delicate scales without beams, gave rise to a complicated system of weights which, although it was not standardised, made it possible to calculate the value of important commodities[4].

Gold dust could not be used for goods of little value, such as retail food and drink. Cowries, the little shells of *Cypraea moneta*, were perfectly suitable for the minor transactions. They spread throughout the whole of Black Africa during the last centuries of the traditional period. They were also used for ornamental and ritual purposes (their shape, suggesting the vulva, associates them with woman and conception), but their success can be explained in terms of their usefulness as money, even when they had to compete with gold and European currencies. Cowries, like metal, do not deteriorate. Whatever happened to them, they always retained their whiteness and polish. Like coins, they could be counted, but they could not be counterfeited or adulterated. Like gold dust, they could be weighed, and even measured by volume. But they were not suitable for modern economic networks. They were subject to constant inflation (very cheap in the Maldive Islands, where they only had to be picked up, they proved very profitable to anyone who transported them elsewhere). In the fifteenth century, they came a long way and were relatively costly to transport. They went from the Indian Ocean to Venice, thence to North Africa, and then by trans-Saharan caravan to the Niger bend. In the nineteenth century the traffic in cowries grew to such proportions, and their value decreased so much, that this too cumbersome form of money was abandoned. Thus in 1901 the British Administration in Uganda ceased to accept cowries in payment for taxes, and destroyed their own stocks[5].

Networks of exchange in modern Africa

There was no break in the field of economic relations for ordinary Africans between traditional and colonial Africa. The circulation of goods outside the markets continued, though it progressively diminished; the economic network expanded considerably and rapidly. One of the explicit objectives of the colonial conquest was, indeed, to sell goods which the new industrial techniques of production had turned out in greater number than European consumption could absorb. Black Africa was a market with millions of potential consumers, but without money. Services, which until then, even more so than goods, had escaped the economic circuit, were now paid for with money. The wages earned, like the surplus in the old days, went partly into the political network (as poll-tax paid to the colonial administration) and partly into the economic network (for purchases in the market). Yet one traditional characteristic remains to this day: for 80 per cent of Africans auto-consumption is still the rule with food.

For most Africans there is complete economic continuity between the colonial and independent periods. Except for regions temporarily isolated by political troubles, where as monetary exchange relations became rarer, the traditional circuits regained their strength, networks of relations between dealers have not been affected by political independence.

Colonial Africa has seen the emergence of large impersonal economic units which were hardly known there before. On this level, the change was a radical one. Before the nineteenth century, certain commercial relations with the outside world gave a foretaste of what was going to happen. The famous trade triangle – cheap, shoddy European goods going to the West African ports, slaves from these ports to the West Indies, sugar and other exotic foods going from America back to Europe – placed Africa in a permanent system of relations constituting a whole over which she had no control, although she was a contributing party. The everyday reality, within this system, was made up of exchanges between dealers corresponding to the elementary model we offer here (an African 'entrepreneur' selling slaves haggled over the price with the captain of a slaver). But the impersonal slave-trade circuit provided the framework of their transactions.

We have already schematised the colonial economic circuit: African raw materials and unskilled labour; European capital and high level personnel; Europe receiving the raw materials and profits, then exporting the finished goods to Africa. Within this firmly established system the multiple societal relations of exchange developed. The African worker and the European overseer who hired him were undoubtedly dealers exchanging services for money, but they operated within a framework which left little margin for negotiation.

The colonial economic system, understood at this level of vast impersonal units, did not come to an end with declarations of national independence. The term 'neo-colonialism', born in the very year (1960 according to Paul Robert's *Dictionnaire de la Langue française*) which marked the end of colonial rule in the political sense, expresses the persistence or even the development of this economic system, in which the young African nations are necessarily involved and are restricted to a role that they can hardly change. As the price of raw materials (always the chief African exports) is, in fact, determined by an agreement between the few rich countries which buy them, it does not rise at the same rate as costs of production. Consequently, to use the words of an African statesman, 'the terms of trade deteriorate'.

Economic relations and power relations

At the beginning of this chapter, we said that exchange and power were antithetical relations, the first being free from any pressure, while the second is based on pressure. But could not the neo-colonial circuit we have just described, and the engagement of an unskilled labour force at low wages by a large mining enterprise, be described as both exchange and power relations? Can we have fallen into the liberal illusion which sees in trade the antidote to authoritarian political régimes? This last idea caught the imagination of the most disinterested sector of European public opinion at the end of the nineteenth century. It saw, in colonial enterprise, the triumphant alliance of the three C's:—Commerce and Christianity bringing Civilisation to a Black Africa which was at the mercy of pagan monarchs and slave-trading Arabs.

The exchange relation certainly does not imply pressure; the two dealers only exchange economic values. But circumstances may give the party who has the goods that the other so desperately needs the chance to inflict a serious deprivation on him. The well-known example is that of the thirsty man who will give away all his riches for water. Circumstances of this kind, which upset the balance between the two parties, were unusual in traditional Africa. This may seem surprising, since material goods were fewer in those days than they are in modern Africa. Certainly they were, but those that were indispensable for the individual and his family were produced by himself and his family. Autarky, while diminishing the circulation of goods, guaranteed to each little production unit all that it needed to subsist, and thus assured its basic economic independence. To this essential security was added the certainty of being able to obtain goods and services by non-economic networks when needed; economic help was given by patriarch or lineage brothers, chief or king, lord or associates in times of need. In the total context of traditional life, people engaged in balanced relations of exchange in which neither side was in a condition of extreme penury.

As monetary exchange spread throughout Africa, each individual depended on it for a greater and greater part of his activities. The villager has preserved the basic security of auto-consumption, but he needs money to pay his taxes, and to buy the manufactured goods he is now accustomed to. The urban African, like all town-dwellers in the industrial age, obtains goods and services with the money he earns by offering other goods and services. In this context, it often happens that various pressures are grafted on to the exchange relation, and that these finally modify the terms of trade. Giving away all one's possessions for a little water when one is dying of thirst has no more than the semblance of an economic transaction. It is not a question of buying a drink, but of saving one's life. In recalling this hackneyed and unreal example, we do not suggest that societal relations of exchange in modern Africa are often associated with unbearable pressures, but rather that its economic network is more likely to channel a relation of power than were those of traditional Africa.

At the level of economic relations between global societies (which is where the neo-colonial system is localised) the small number of inter-acting units makes the situation clearer still. A collectivity has fewer options open to it than an individual dealer: a developing country often does not have any real choice. It only has one buyer for a given product. In this context, the economic relationship is the support of probable pressures.

Thus the network where economic values are exchanged in return for other values of the same kind, where the principles governing a market economy were discovered, where, by definition, irrational forces alien to supply and demand are excluded, can also be a vehicle of power relations: the vehicle and the veil at the same time.

Acknowledgments

Acknowledgment is due to the following for the illustrations (the number refers to the page on which the illustration appears): 15, 28 (bottom), 43, 47, 60–1, 76, 129, 150, 163 (top), 180, 183 (top and bottom) Afrique Photo, Paris; 28 (top), 67 (top), 168, 171 J. Allan Cash; 29 Kenya Information Service, London; 67 (bottom), 71, 75, 79 (Peter Larsen), 106–7, 116, 117, 133 (Paul Almasy), 144 Camera Press Ltd; 100 Photographie Bulloz; 218, 221 Paul Popper; 219 (three photographs), 222 Pierre Ichac. The following photographs were supplied by the author: 11, 35, 51, 52, 78, 91, 92, 98, 102, 111, 113, 121, 149, 155, 163 (bottom), 169, 177, 193, 199, 232–2, 237.
The maps and figures were drawn by Design Practitioners Ltd.

Notes

These notes give only the name of the author, date of publication and page reference. Full references will be found in the Bibliography.

1 THE APPROACH TO AFRICAN SOCIÉTIES

1 Senghor, 1967.
2 Maquet, 1967.
3 Murdock, 1959.

2 POWER

1 Russell, 1938: 25.
2 Dahl, 1968: 407–10. ˆ
3 Weber, 1957: 152.
4 Lasswell, 1948: 12.
5 Maquet, 1954: 176–9.
6 Russell, 1938: 12–13.

3 DESCENT FROM THE SAME ANCESTOR

1 Maquet, 1962 and 1968.
2 Balandier, 1967: 43.
3 Mair, 1962: 18.
4 Balandier, 1967: 43.
5 Parsons, 1966: 9.

4 CONTRACTING AN ALLIANCE

1 RAI, 1951: 110.
2 Comhaire-Sylvain, 1968.

5 GOVERNMENT

1 Balandier, 1967: 50–2.
2 Radcliffe-Brown, 1940: xiv.
3 Middleton and Tait, 1958: 1.
4 Schapera, 1956: 218.
5 Balandier, 1967: 43.
6 Polanyi, 1968: 153–4.
7 Balandier, 1967: 47.

6 REPETITIVE AND DYNAMIC MODELS

1 Balandier, 1967: 226.
2 Radcliff-Brown, 1952; Malinowski, 1947.

7 INEQUALITY

1 Dumont, 1967.
2 Kagame, 1959; Vansina, 1962.
3 Maquet, 1954: 173–4.
4 Beattie, 1960: 11–12.
5 Murdock, 1967: 66.
6 The most useful and complete bibliographies on the Great Lakes societies are in Chave Fallers, 1960; Taylor, 1962; D'Hertefelt, Trouwborst and Scherer, 1962. After 1962, see notably Oliver and Mathew, 1963; Lemarchand, 1966.
7 Maquet, 1964.
8 Maquet, 1962: 250.
9 Kimble, 1960: 1, 98; Barbé, 1964: 16.
10 Oberg, 1940: 122.

8 DEPENDENCE RELATIONS

1 Maquet, 1961: 129–33.
2 Oberg, 1940: 128; Taylor, 1962: 109.
3 D'Hertefelt, Trouwborst and Scherer, 1962: 120, 151.
4 D'Hertefelt et al., 1962: 178, 205.
5 Ganshof, 1957: 11.
6 Bloch, 1949: 2: 249.

7 Nikitin, 1966: 32–4.
8 Bloch, 1949; Stephenson, 1956; Coulborn, 1956; Boutruche, 1957; Maquet, 1961b.
9 Ganshof, 1957: 16. For other uses of the term *client* in the African domain, see Lombard, 1960: 11; Mair, 1961.
10 Coulborn, 1956: 4.
11 Oliver and Mathew, 1963: 185.
12 Lombard, 1966.

9 ASSOCIATION
1 Zehan, 1960; Mercier, 1968; Ichac, 1968.
2 Mercier, 1968: 52.
3 Turnbull, 1961.

10 EXCHANGE OF GOODS
1 Bohannan and Dalton, 1965: 6.
2 *Ibid*: 11.
3 Maquet, Emma, 1968: 175.
4 Paulme, 1968: 304, 335.
5 Polanyi, 1966: 176.

This bibliography is a complete list of all authors mentioned in the end notes. Titles marked with an asterisk are recommended as being particularly useful for further reading on the topics discussed in this book.

*BALANDIER, Georges, 1967: *Anthropologie politique*. Paris: Presses universitaires de France.

BALANDIER, Georges and Jacques MAQUET, dir., 1968: *Dictionnaire des civilisations africaines*. Paris: Hazan.

BARBÉ, Raymond, 1964: *Les classes sociales en Afrique noire*. Paris: Économie et politique.

BEATTIE, John, 1960: *Bunyoro, An African Kingdom*. New York: Holt, Rinehart & Winston.

BLOCH, Marc, 1939–1940: *La société féodale*. Paris: Albin Michel. 2 vol; *Feudal Society*, trans. L. A. Manyon, Chicago University Press, 1961.

*BOHANNAN, Paul and George DALTON, eds., 1962: *Markets in Africa*. North Western University Press; 1965: Garden City, N.Y.: Doubleday.

BOUTRUCHE, Robert, 1959: *Seigneurie et féodalité, le premier âge des liens d'homme à homme*. Paris: Aubier.

CHAVE FALLERS, Margaret, 1960: *The Eastern Lacustrine Bantu*. London: International African Institute.

COMHAIRE-SYLVAIN, Suzanne, 1968: *Femmes de Kinshasa*. Paris: Mouton.

*COULBORN, Rushton, ed., 1956: *Feudalism in History*. Princeton, N.J.: Princeton University Press.

*DAHL, Robert A., 1968: 'Power'. *International Encyclopedia of the Social Sciences* ed. by David L. Sills. New York: Macmillan & Free Press. 12: 405–415.

DUMONT, Louis, 1967: *Homo hierarchicus, essai sur le système des castes*. Paris: Gallimard; *Homo Hierarchicus, The Caste System and its applications*, trs. Mark Sainsbury, Weidenfeld and Nicolson, 1970.

*FORTES, M. and E. E. EVANS-PRITCHARD, eds., 1940: *African Political Systems*. London: Oxford University Press (for the International African Institute); New York, 1955.

GANSHOF, F. L., 1944: *Qu'est-ce que la féodalité?* Bruxelles: Office de publicité; *Feudalism*, trans. P. Grierson, London, New York: Longmans, 1952.

d'HERTEFELT, M., A. A. TROUWBORST and J. H. SCHERER, 1962: *Les anciens royaumes de zone interlacustre méridionale*. Tervuren: Musée royal de l'Afrique centrale; also published as Ethnographic Survey of Africa, East Central Africa, pt. 14.

ICHAC, Pierre, 1968: 'Hommes-lions et hommes-panthères'. *Dictionnaire des civilisations africaines* edd. Georges Balandier and Jacques Maquet. Paris: Hazan. 206–208.

KAGAME, Alexis, 1959: *La notion de génération appliquée à la généalogie dynastique et à l'histoire du Rwanda des Xe-XIe siècles à nos jours.* Bruxelles: Académie royale des sciences coloniales.

KIMBLE, George H.T., 1960: *Tropical Africa.* New York: Twentieth Century Fund. 2 vol.; 1962, abridged edn., 2 vol., New York: Doubleday.

*KRADER, Lawrence, 1968: *Formation of the State.* Englewood Cliffs, N.J.: Prentice-Hall.

LASSWELL, H.D., 1948: *Power and Personality.* New York: W.W.Norton.

LEMARCHAND, René, 1966: 'Power and Stratification in Rwanda'. *Cahiers d'études africaines,* Paris. 6, 4(24): 592–610.

LÉVI-STRAUSS, Claude, 1949: *Les structures élémentaires de la parenté.* Paris: Presses universitaires de France; reissued 1967, Paris: Mouton; *The Elementary structures of Kinship,* revised edn., trans. R.Needham *et al.,* London: Eyre & Spottiswoode; Boston; Beacon Press, 1969.

LOMBARD, Jacques, 1960: 'La vie politique dans une ancienne société de type féodal: les Bariba du Dahomey'. *Cahiers d'études africaines,* Paris. 1, 3(3): 5–45.

LOMBARD, Jacques, 1965: *Structures de type 'féodal' en Afrique noire.* Paris: Mouton.

MAIR, Lucy P., 1961: 'Clientship in East Africa'. *Cahiers d'études africaines,* Paris. 2, 2(6): 315–325.

*MAIR, Lucy P., 1962: *Primitive Government.* Harmondsworth, Middlesex, Baltimore: Penguin Books.

MALINOWSKI, Bronislaw, 1931: 'Culture'. *Encyclopaedia of the Social Sciences.* New York: Macmillan. 4: 621–646.

MAQUET, Emma, 1968: 'Fer'. *Dictionnaire des civilisation africaines* edd. Georges Balandier and Jacques Maquet. Paris: Hazan. 174–177.

MAQUET, Jacques, 1954: 'The Kingdom of Ruanda'. *African Worlds* ed. by Daryll Forde. London: Oxford University Press (for the International African Institute). 164–189.

MAQUET, Jacques, 1961a: *The Premise of Inequality in Ruanda.* London: Oxford University Press (for the International African Institute).

MAQUET, Jacques, 1961b: 'Une hypothèse pour l'étude des féodalités africaines'. *Cahiers d'études africaines,* Paris. 2, 2(6): 292–314.

MAQUET, Jacques, 1962: *Afrique, les civilisations noires*. Paris: Horizons de France.

MAQUET, Jacques, 1964: 'La participation de la classe paysanne au mouvement d'indépendance du Rwanda'. *Cahiers d'études africaines*, Paris. 4, 4(16): 552–568.

MAQUET, Jacques, 1967: *Africanité traditionnelle et moderne*. Paris: Présence africaine.

*MAQUET, Jacques, 1968: 'African Society: Sub-Saharan Africa'. *International Encyclopedia of the Social Sciences* ed. David L. Sills. New York: Macmillan & Free Press. 1: 137–155.

MERCIER, Paul, 1968: 'Associations'. *Dictionnaire des civilisations africaines* edd. Georges Balandier and Jacques Maquet. Paris: Hazan. 50–52.

*MIDDLETON, John and David TAIT, edd., 1958: *Tribes Without Rulers*. London: Routledge & Kegan Paul.

*MIDDLETON, John and Ronald COHEN, edd., 1967: *Comparative Political Systems*. National History Press for American Museum of Natural History.

MURDOCK, George P., 1959: *Africa, Its Peoples and Their Culture History*. New York: McGraw-Hill.

MURDOCK, George P., 1967: *Ethnographic Atlas*. Pittsburgh: University of Pittsburgh Press.

NIKITIN, P., 1966: *Principes d'économie politique*. Moscow: Éditions de Moscou; Fundamentals of Political Economy, trans. Violet Dutt and M. Saifulin, Moscow: Foreign Languages Publishing House, 1963.

OBERG, K., 1940: 'The Kingdom of Ankole in Uganda'. *African Political Systems* edd. M. Fortes and E. E. Evans-Pritchard. London: Oxford University Press (for the International African Institute). 121–162; New York 1955.

OLIVER, Roland and Gervase MATHEW, 1963: *History of East Africa*. London: Oxford University Press. Vol. 1.

PARSONS, Talcott, 1966: *Societies: evolutionary and comparative perspectives*, Englewood Cliffs, N.J.: Prentice-Hall.

PAULME, Denise, 1968: 'Or', 'Poids'. *Dictionnaire des civilisations africaines* edd. Georges Balandier and Jacques Maquet. Paris: Hazan. 304–306, 335–336.

POLANYI, Karl, 1966: *Dahomey and the Slave Trade. An Analysis of an Archaic Economy*. Seattle: University of Washington Press.

POLANYI, Karl, 1968: *Primitive, Archaic and Modern Economies* ed. George Dalton. Garden City, N.Y.: Doubleday.

RADCLIFFE-BROWN, A. R., 1940: 'Preface'. *African Political Systems* edd. M. Fortes and E. E. Evans-Pritchard. London: Oxford University Press (for the International African Institute) xi–xxiii.

RADCLIFFE-BROWN, A. R., 1952: *Structures and Function in Primitive Society*. London: Cohen and West.

ROYAL ANTHROPOLOGICAL INSTITUTE OF GREAT BRITAIN AND IRELAND, 1951: *Notes and Queries on Anthropology* (6th edn.). London: Routledge & Kegan Paul.

RUSSELL, Bertrand, 1938: *Power: a new social analysis*. New York: W. W. Norton; London: Allen & Unwin.

SCHAPERA, Isaac, 1956: *Government and Politics in Tribal Societies*. London: Watts; 1967; New York: Schocken Books.

SENGHOR, Léopold Sédar, 1967: *Les fondements de l'africanité ou négritude et arabité*. Paris: Présence africaine.

STEPHENSON, Carl, 1956: *Mediaeval Feudalism*. Ithaca, N.Y.: Cornell University Press.

TAYLOR, Brian K., 1962: *The Western Lacustrine Bantu*. London: International African Institute.

*TUMIN, Melvin M., 1967: *Social Stratification, The Forms and Functions of Inequality*. Englewood Cliffs, N.J.: Prentice-Hall.

TURNBULL, Colin M., 1961: *The Forest People*. London: Chatto & Windus; New York: Simon & Schuster.

VANSINA, Jan, 1962: *L'évolution du royaume rwanda des origines à 1900*. Bruxelles: Académie royale des Sciences d'outremer.

WEBER, Max, 1957: *The Theory of Social and Economic Organization* ed. Talcott Parsons. Glencoe, Ill.: Free Press; London: Hodge, 1947.

ZAHAN, Dominique, 1960: *Sociétiés d'initiation Bambara*. Paris: Mouton.

252

Some books published or in preparation

Economics and Social Studies

The World Cities
Peter Hall, *Reading*

The Economics of Underdeveloped Countries
Jagdish Bhagwati, *MIT*

Development Planning
Jan Tinbergen, *Rotterdam*

Human Communication
J. L. Aranguren, *Madrid*

Education in the Modern World
John Vaizey, *London*

Soviet Economics
Michael Kaser, *Oxford*

Decisive Forces in World Economics
J. L. Sampedro, *Madrid*

Key Issues in Criminology
Roger Hood and Richard Sparks, *Cambridge*

Population and History
E. A. Wrigley, *Cambridge*

Woman, Society and Change
Evelyne Sullerot, *Paris*

Power and Society in Africa
Jacques Maquet, *Paris*

History

The Emergence of Greek Democracy
W. G. Forrest, *Oxford*

Muhammad and the Conquests of Islam
Francesco Gabrieli, *Rome*

The Civilisation of Charlemagne
Jacques Boussard, *Poitiers*

Humanism in the Renaissance
S. Dresden, *Leyden*

The Rise of Toleration
Henry Kamen, *Warwick*

Science and Change 1500-1700
Hugh Kearney, *Sussex*

The Left in Europe
David Caute, *London*

The Rise of the Working Class
Jürgen Kuczynski, *Berlin*

Chinese Communism
Robert North, *Stanford*

The Italian City Republics
Daniel Waley, *London*

Rome: The Story of an Empire
J. P. V. D. Balsdon, *Oxford*

Cosmology
Jean Charon

The Arts

Twentieth Century Music
H. H. Stuckenschmidt, *Berlin*

Art Nouveau
S. Tschudi Madsen, *Oslo*

Palaeolithic Cave Art
P. J. Ucko and A. Rosenfeld, *London*

Expressionism
John Willett, *London*

Language and Literature

Two Centuries of French Literature
Raymond Picard, *Paris*

Russian Writers and Society 1825-1904
Ronald Hingley, *Oxford*

Satire
Matthew Hodgart, *Sussex*